Ex Libris

JEFFREY RAYMOND

1988

MY GARDEN

MY GARDEN

A Journal

for Gardening Around the Year

by LOUISE MURPHY

Illustrated by Lisa C. Ernst

CHARLES SCRIBNER'S SONS, NEW YORK

*For Christopher, Virginia, and
curious children everywhere*

Text copyright © 1980 Louise Murphy

Illustrations copyright © 1980 Lisa Campbell Ernst

Library of Congress Cataloging in Publication Data

Murphy, Louise, 1943-
My garden.

SUMMARY: A journal with weekly entries for
gardening around the year.
1. Gardening—Juvenile literature. 2. Natural
history—Juvenile literature. 3. Tales.
[1. Gardening] I. Title.
SB457.M87   635   79-29650
ISBN 0-684-16486-8

1 3 5 7 9 11 13 15 17 19 F/C 20 18 16 14 12 10 8 6 4 2

Printed in the United States of America

CONTENTS

JANUARY

The First Week / 10
Gardens · You · Keeping a Journal · Snow · Dormancy

The Second Week / 16
Hard Work and Hard Times · Weeds · Light

The Third Week / 22
Water · Blue Celery · One Who Lives Alone—An Indian Tale
Corn · Special Food

The Fourth Week / 26
Animals · Dirt · Birds

FEBRUARY

The First Week / 32
Your Kitchen

The Second Week / 34
Moon Stories · Moon Planting · Your Moon

The Third Week / 38
The Unhappy Mother—A Greek Myth · Weather · Planting

The Fourth Week / 43
Onion Prints · Indoor Garden

MARCH

The First Week / 46
Season of the Senses · Spring Feasting

The Second Week / 48
How the Earth Began—A North American Indian Legend
Compost—and How to Make It

The Third Week / 51
Foraging · Trees · A Contest—A Greek Myth · Spider Art

The Fourth Week / 56
Time to Begin

APRIL
The First Week / 60
Planning Your Garden

The Second Week / 62
Planting · Onions · Garlic

The Third Week / 65
The Princess and the Pea—A Fairy Tale · Peas · Carrots

The Fourth Week / 69
Spring Fun · Raphanus Sativus

MAY
The First Week / 74
The Silly Woman—A Cochiti Indian Story · Squash

The Second Week / 77
Tomatoes · Lettuce · The Dread Snail

The Third Week / 82
The Gift—A Caddo Indian Story · Beans · Cucumbers

The Fourth Week / 85
Clytie—A Greek Myth · Corn · Sunflowers

JUNE
The First Week / 90
The All-Purpose Plants

The Second Week / 93
Patience · Food for Impatience · Weeding · Indoor Mulching

The Third Week / 97
How Do They Do It? · Bees · Looking

The Fourth Week / 102
Worms

JULY

The First Week / 106
The Immortal Toad—A Chinese Legend · Toads, Good or Bad?
Peas and Carrots

The Second Week / 109
Silly Jack—An Old Irish Tale · Jack-O'-Lanterns

The Third Week / 114
The Beautiful Maiden—An American Indian Story · Water

The Fourth Week / 117
A Good Bug · Ladybugs · The Praying Mantis

AUGUST

The First Week / 124
The Peaceful Tribe · The Ocean and the Land · Hungry Burros
Plants and Seaweed

The Second Week
The Giant Turnip—A Russian Tale · Turnips

The Third Week / 130
How Plants Eat · Water · Zucchini

The Fourth Week / 134
The Green Cup Legend · Green · Clubs

SEPTEMBER

The First Week / 138
Autumn · A Strange Plant

The Second Week / 141
Circles · Connections

The Third Week / 143
Checklists

The Fourth Week / 144
Books and Catalogues · Free Goodies

OCTOBER

The First Week / 148
Getting Ready · Leaf Magic

The Second Week / 150
Harvesting

The Third Week / 152
Pumpkin Picking · Carving a Pumpkin

The Fourth Week / 154
The End · Tools · Moments

Index / 158

JANUARY

And God said, "Behold, I have given you every herb bearing seed which is upon the face of all the earth."

—Genesis 1:29

JANUARY

THE FIRST WEEK

GARDENS

Once upon a time, there were no gardens on the earth. The earth revolved around the sun and seasons passed. Winter brought snow and rain, summers were often hot, but no one planted a garden. Strange reptiles and mammals lived during these times. They ate the plants, fought, lay in the sun, created more of their kind, and died, but none of them planted a seed. The earth was waiting for the first gardener.

Then the strangest mammal of all began to walk over the earth. Ten, twenty, thirty million years ago this mammal stood up on its hind legs and learned how to use axes, knives, and fire to trap and kill animals for food. These mammals were men and women. They were human beings, but none of them planted a garden.

Gardens take time. It takes days for the seeds to germinate in the earth, weeks for the seeds to grow roots and stems and leaves, and more weeks until the plants can be eaten.

Twenty million years ago, men and women had no time for raising plants. Sometimes the weather was much hotter than it is now. Sometimes great sheets of ice miles thick would creep down over part of the earth.

Men and women lived through all these years by wandering. If the animals moved south, then women and men would pick up their babies and their tools and move south too. The men hunted every day for animals to kill. It was hard for the women to hunt when they were pregnant or when they were carrying their babies. They couldn't put the babies down and leave them while they hunted, but the women could carry baskets and sacks with them and gather berries, roots, and plants while they cared for the children. When the animals and plants grew scarce, the people moved on.

Gardeners are not wanderers. It was a long time before people could stop wandering enough to grow a garden.

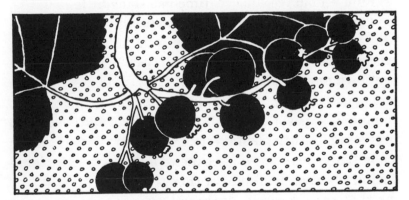

YOU

Today you are going to do something that people did not do for twenty million years. You are going to become a gardener, a farmer. A gardener is a person who plants seeds and bulbs and roots and then manages them. Gardeners and farmers manage their plants so that people can eat better and feed their bodies. Some gardeners raise flowers, and the colors and shapes of the flowers feed the hearts and souls of everyone who sees their beauty. Every part of a person needs food of some sort, and gardeners grow the food.

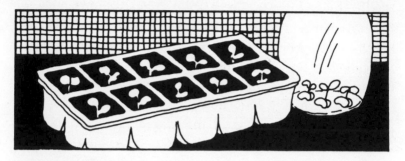

Find an old ice-cube tray, or use some little jars.

Take some beans, any sort—red, black, black-eyed peas, mung beans, alfalfa seeds—and put two beans or seeds in each compartment of the ice-cube tray. Put two beans where every ice cube should go. If you are using jars, put two or three beans in each jar. Then pour enough water over the beans to cover them and cover the tray and jars with plastic wrap. Put the tray and jars on a shelf in your room where they won't be in the sunlight during the day. Look at the beans every day. Describe the changes you see or draw pictures of the beans each day for twelve days. Keep them wet. Take care not to knock them over. You are now a gardener.

KEEPING A JOURNAL

A journal is a record of events. Many people have kept journals, and they can be fun to write in and then read later. You can keep a journal about gardening. It can be a notebook or a tablet of paper, any size that you want. Big pages are nice, because then you can clip in pressed leaves and flowers easily.

You can write about your experiments in growing seeds—for instance, the experiment that was just described—draw pictures and keep lists of birds that you see, press leaves between waxed paper and keep them in your journal, or draw a picture of your garden. If you like to write poems or stories, you might try to make up some about your garden and the things that you see in it. The whole world is alive and moving and fascinating to watch and be part of. Keeping a journal is one way of saying what you have seen during the gardening year.

SNOW

If you live in Miami or San Diego, you may never have seen snow. When I was a little girl, there was always a beautiful morning in winter when I would wake up and see something different in my bedroom. The light would be very bright and bounce off the walls. It would be so clear and white that I would have to shut my eyes until I remembered. Then I would jump out from under the blankets and, sure enough, there would be snow on the ground outside, bouncing the sun into my room. I knew that snow smelled nice and made the air much brighter, but I didn't know what snow was for.

Snow is really a blanket for the earth. It lies in a heavy mass on the soil and leaves and keeps the heat of the earth tight against all the roots and bulbs that are under the dirt. It is like the insulation that people roll out in big strips on their attic floor to keep the warmth down in their house.

In the spring the snow melts and waters the earth so that seeds will grow. It takes warmth and water to make your beans grow. The snow gives the earth water so that the growing can begin.

Snowflakes are tiny drops of water that have frozen. Each snowflake is made of even smaller ice crystals that have stuck together. When it is very, very cold, the snowflakes are smaller because the crystals of ice can't stick together well in great cold. Springtime snows often have huge snowflakes because it is warmer then and the ice crystals stick together.

Ice crystals are very beautiful. Every crystal has six sides. This shape is called a hexagon, and each hexagon is a little different from every other hexagon. If every crystal of snow were as big as we are, it would be like standing in a shower of white jewels when it snows.

DORMANCY

The word "dormant" comes from very old French and English words that mean "asleep." So when we say that a flower bush or a tree is "dormant," we mean that they are asleep.

Look outside at the trees in your yard or go to a park where there are trees. Some of the trees have no leaves in January. Their branches are still and look dead with no green leaves and stems rustling, but they are not really dead at all. They are asleep during the winter cold. Pick one tree out that has no leaves on its branches. Look at the branches and the tips of the branches. See the lumps? Watch this tree every week for the next three or four months. You will see it wake up.

During the summer the tree makes food when the sun shines on its leaves. The food is stored in the tree after the leaves turn brown and blow away. Then the tree has food for the winter. It can live on this food until the weather is warm and new leaves grow.

Some trees don't lose their leaves. They are called evergreens. Pine and fir trees don't have leaves. They

have needles instead. These trees don't sleep all winter. They get through the winter by using less food than they do in the warm summer. You might say that evergreen trees take a long nap in the winter, but they never go to sleep.

THE SECOND WEEK

HARD WORK AND HARD TIMES

No one knows exactly when the first person planted seeds and made a garden. We can't even tell if planting and harvesting, making gardens, began in Europe, Africa, China, North America, South America, Australia, or on the islands scattered over the earth.

First men and women tamed wild animals and learned to raise sheep and goats, pigs and birds for food. This was a big change from being hunters. Now the families wandered with their animals, looking for food for the goats and sheep. The animal skins were used for clothes, for tents, for blankets and the meat was eaten.

Women wove cloth from the animals' woolly coats and used the animals' milk to feed the children and for cooking.

About seven thousand years ago, people all over the world discovered how to plant seeds and harvest the plants that grew up. The first gardeners used sticks to make holes in the soil. Then they dropped seeds in the holes and hoped for enough rain and sun to grow the plants.

Every country grew different plants. Countries with lots of low, wet land grew rice because this crop needed a lot of water. First India grew rice and then the idea spread to China and most of the east. In Mexico they grew maize, which was the first corn, and they grew peppers and avocado trees. These plants needed warm weather to grow.

In Europe the people had problems with the forests. There were huge forests that covered hundreds of miles, and the people couldn't plant their crops because the trees and brush would choke out the little seedlings. Cutting down all the trees would have taken too long, so these women and men learned how to burn big patches of forest by setting parts of the forest on fire. Then the land was bare. The sun could reach the ground, and seeds were planted.

In Egypt the weather was very hot, and the plants didn't always get enough rain to grow. The huge Nile river flows through Egypt, and smart farmers learned to dig ditches that went from the river bank into their fields. The river water flowed into the ditches and watered the growing plants. This is called irrigation.

In the Netherlands, the ocean covered acres and acres of land in low, salty flats. The people needed more land for their crops, so they dug ditches to drain off the salt water, built walls to hold the water back, and stole land from the sea itself.

The people weren't always so successful when they gardened and farmed. Six hundred years ago there was very bad weather in Europe. The crops died, and thousands of people starved because there was no way then to can and freeze food for emergencies. Then a terrible sickness called the Black Death spread from village to village and many people died. (We know now that the Black Death was bubonic plague.) There were floods and wars.

The people were not able to plant their fields because many of them were sick or fighting in the wars. Sometimes men would march right over the fields in a village or burn the crops. Because of all these problems many people were hungry and couldn't harvest their crops.

You can't have a garden when there is a war being fought in your own backyard. Bad weather and wars are hard on gardens and fields of plants. Gardeners like peace and good weather so their plants can grow.

WEEDS

When people first began to garden, they probably didn't think about whether a plant should be called a weed. When the people of a village in Mexico planted a field with squash seeds, they wanted to get lots of squash to eat. If some other seeds blew into the field, then the people of the village would pull them out when they grew. They didn't want any other plants taking water, sun and soil away from the squash plants.

Most people think of weeds as ugly, useless plants, but weeds also serve many purposes in nature. Weeds with long roots bring minerals up from deep in the soil so other plants with shallow roots can use the minerals. Weeds can hold the soil in place with their roots so it won't be washed or blown away. When weeds die, they add their organic matter to the soil and become part of the earth's natural compost. Some weeds, such as thistles, are used for decoration, and leaves of the dandelion, when picked in early spring, are delicious in salads although it is considered a weed by most people.

Sometimes a plant is considered a weed until someone discovers how to use it for medicine or food. Some

plants are used by a lot of people at one time and then are not used much for hundreds of years.

Marigold plants have lovely flowers. Years ago, people stirred marigold flowers into soups and ate the yellow petals, but we don't eat them now. I don't know why.

Most people now hate to see dandelion plants growing in the middle of their lawns. Dandelions are weeds when they grow in the grassy lawns. But dandelion flowers are very beautiful, and the seeds, arranged in a circle of air and fluff on the stem, are like a star against the grass. Other people love dandelions because the new green leaves are tasty in salads, and still other people like to make dandelion wine from the plant.

I loved the clover that grew in my front yard when I was young. I could pick mounds of it and sit on hot days under the trees making long clover chains by knotting the stems together. Some people spray poison chemicals on their grass to kill the clover, but clover can be much more interesting than grass. Farmers like clover because the cows love to eat it, and anyone who keeps bees likes to plant a field of clover so the bees will make sweet clover honey.

It all depends on how you look at a plant. Some people's weeds are other people's flowers and food.

LIGHT

Plants need light to grow. The easiest way to give a plant light is to plant it in a sunny place or put the pot in a sunny window. If there isn't much sun coming through your windows, you can buy special lights and hang them over your plants or borrow a sunnier window from a neighbor.

Try an experiment this week. Take some of the beans you sprouted last week and plant them in little pots or jars. If the ground outside is too wet or frozen to dig up, you can buy small sacks of potting soil at a nursery or supermarket.

Put some dirt in each pot and bury one of your beans about an inch under the dirt. Then put the pots in a dark closet or in a box where no light can get in. Don't forget to keep the soil damp.

If you want to try a more interesting experiment, put about one-third of the beans in a dark place, one-third of them on a shelf by a sunny window where they will get lots of light, and one-third in a room where the sun won't touch them. Don't move the pots at all when you water the beans.

Watch all three sets of beans. What do their new leaves look like? Do the leaves and stems in each pot all turn in one direction?

When the plants get bigger, try turning the pots and watch the leaves and the stems turn themselves around.

Take the plants out of the closet or box in two weeks. Put them first in a room with light and no sun, and then move them into the sun in a few days. Do they change? Leave one pot in the closet. What happens in a few weeks?

What you are seeing is called phototropism, which means the movement of a plant toward or away from the light.

THE THIRD WEEK

WATER

Plants also need water to grow. Maybe you forgot to water your bean plants and found that out already.

Try doing this experiment and see what happens. Take one bean plant and put it out by itself. Don't water it at all for two weeks. Let the soil dry out.

Take another bean plant and put it in a bowl that is large enough to hold the entire pot. Fill the bowl with water so the bean plant's pot and soil are covered with the water. Keep the rest of your beans moist but not wet. Which plant looks the healthiest in a week?

BLUE CELERY

Try another experiment with plants and water. Take a large celery stalk. Cut a piece about one-inch long off the bottom of the stalk, but leave all the leaves on the plant.

Add a lot of red or blue food coloring to about a half-cup of water in a glass or clear jar. Make the water a bright color. Stick the cut end of the celery stalk into the colored water (the leafy end should be out of the water) and let it sit a few hours or overnight. The next morning, you can see that the celery has "drunk" some of the water.

This is called hydrotropism, or how a plant grows toward or away from water.

One Who Lives Alone—An Indian Tale

Once upon a time there was a man named One Who Lives Alone. He had lived all his life alone with no wife or children or family around him. One night a beautiful young woman with long blond hair woke him up. One Who Lives Alone loved her and begged her to stay with him forever. She promised to never leave if he would do exactly what she told him.

One Who Lives Alone agreed to do whatever

she said, but he was frightened when he heard her commands.

"Set the field across the creek on fire," the fair-haired woman said, "and when the sun has gone down, take me by my pale hair and drag me over the field."

How could One Who Lives Alone do this? He loved the maiden and did not want to hurt her, but she said he must do it. She would leave if he did not do this thing.

Smiling mysteriously, the maiden promised that a "plant like a grass" would grow up in the field and One Who Lives Alone would be able to eat the seeds of the plant. She told him that the seeds would make his hunger go away forever.

One Who Lives Alone did as the strange maiden said, and from the burned field sprang hundreds of corn plants the next day.

The maiden still hasn't left One Who Lives Alone, because in every ear of corn, wrapped in a warm blanket around the kernels, is a piece of her silky yellow hair.

CORN

"One Who Lives Alone" is one of many stories that the Indian people tell about how they first planted corn. If you take one kernel of corn off a dry corncob and plant the kernel, it grows and makes a plant with several ears of corn on it. Each of these ears of corn have hundreds of separate kernels of corn.

When the Indian people in North, South, and Central America learned to plant corn, they saw what a great miracle and mystery is in each kernel of corn. Every year kernels of corn were planted in the ground, and each kernel that grew made hundreds and hundreds of other kernels.

The Indians were grateful to the corn plants and treated the corn very respectfully. Indian children were often taught to care for the plants and were told that to waste the corn would be very ungrateful of them.

The Indians ate the corn fresh. They ate the corn silk, too, because it is also a nutritious food. The children sucked the sweet sap from the stalks of certain corn plants like they were eating candy. Much of the corn was dried and ground up for cornmeal.

Corn was used as a medicine and as a part of religious ceremonies. When babies were born, tiny dabs of fine cornmeal were sometimes put on the babies' mouths.

The Navaho and Zuni Indians ground kernels of corn and used them to make pictures. The corn kernels were separated according to their color, ground up, and poured onto smooth sand to make designs. Each color meant something different. Yellow corn was used to represent the earth. Red corn was the north, white corn the east, and blue corn was the west. Black corn meant the world underneath our earth.

SPECIAL FOOD

Corn was so important to the Indians that they used it in every part of their life. Perhaps you use some food in a special way, or you eat special foods on holidays and birthdays. Perhaps you eat some special food when you celebrate a holy day in your religion. Maybe your family has one favorite food that they eat often.

Write or tell a story about your family's favorite food. It can be a serious story or a funny story.

Draw some pictures of the foods that are special to you. The pictures and story can be part of a journal if you are keeping one.

THE FOURTH WEEK

ANIMALS

If you were a Creek Indian child who lived two hundred years ago, you would have slept outside all summer. You would have taken your blanket and laid down at night next to your family's bean field. As you lay there, watching the stars, feeling sleepy, you would have heard the bean plants rustling in the wind. Then you might have heard another rustle, the rustle as a fat raccoon tore the tender leaves and pods off a plant for its dinner or the light tap of a hungry deer. Up you would have jumped, throwing rocks and shouting, scaring the deer and raccoons out of your family's garden.

There are a lot of hungry animals in the world besides

people, and they like gardens as much as we do. There are also animals that may not eat your plants but can damage them if they get into the garden. If your garden is outside this summer, you may have to put a fence around it to keep rabbits and dogs out. I know a woman who built a fence around her garden and then planted a row of carrots outside the fence for the rabbits. She said that the rabbits took all the carrots outside the fence and never took one carrot from inside the garden. Maybe they were grateful for the present.

DIRT

Do you like to get dirty? I do. I like to get really muddy. If you go barefoot when it rains, the mud oozes up between your toes. It feels just great, like the earth is alive and moving under your feet.

What is dirt? It's a lot of things. The soil in your yard,

the soil in parks and on farms is made up of hundreds of different parts. It can take 500 years to make one inch of soil on the earth's surface.

Soil starts with rocks. The sun and rain and wind wear the rocks down. They crack and crumble and break up into tiny pieces. These pieces get mixed up with dead leaves, grass, sticks, and rain water. Then worms and grubs begin to live in the soil. Bacteria and molds so tiny that your eyes can't see them grow in the soil. This mixture of dead leaves and vegetable stuff, rocks, worms, and even dead animals makes a rich blanket that covers the earth.

Some parts of the earth are good to grow things on. Some aren't. Deserts are too dry for most plants and too sandy. Sometimes the land next to the ocean is too salty for plants to grow in.

When you plant your seeds, you are going to have to look at your dirt really hard. If it isn't good for plants, you can learn to make it better.

BIRDS

There are birds everywhere. There are birds far out over the ocean. There are birds in forests and over deserts. There are birds in city streets and in your own backyard.

Try keeping a bird journal. Write down a description or draw a picture of some of the birds you can see in your neighborhood. Watch the birds.

Look at their shape, their claws, their beaks, their color. Notice how they fly, or walk. You may want to get a book out of the library that shows pictures and names for the birds in your part of the country.

Birdhouses

Birds can be good and bad for gardeners. Like most things in life, they are never all good or all pesky. Birds can eat your corn or strawberries up before you can pick them, but birds also kill billions of bugs that can kill your plants too. If we didn't have birds, the world would be covered with bugs, and the bugs are hungry too. Birds are one of the best ways for gardeners to get rid of bugs, and some people build birdhouses just so the birds will come to their yard every year.

If you want a birdhouse, you have to put it out now, but don't be surprised if the birds don't take to it right away. Some birds don't like new birdhouses. They like a house that smells like the outdoors.

A good birdhouse is an old plastic bleach bottle with a molded handle. Wash it out really well so it doesn't smell like bleach. Then you can paint it dark green or brown with waterproof outdoor paint. Cut a hole for the bird's door about three or four inches from the bottom of the bottle. Make it small, about one or one-and-a-half inches around. Make another very little hole under the door and stick a peg or stick in this hole for a perch. A dab of waterproof glue or epoxy on the perch should keep it secure. The bird can land on this perch and look around before it pops into the house. It is the bird's front porch.

Punch a few small holes in the bottom so any rain can drain out and the birds won't be sitting in a puddle. Hang the bottle up with a wire through the handle where it will be high enough so cats won't get it. You may need some help from someone with a ladder.

If the birds don't use it this year, leave it up. They may use it next year.

FEBRUARY

In the ocean of
  the sky
Wave-clouds are
  rising.
The ship of the
  moon
Seems to be row-
  ing along
Through a forest
  of stars.

—Kakinomoto no
  Asomi Hitomaro
  about 735 A.D.

FEBRUARY

THE FIRST WEEK

YOUR KITCHEN

Most kitchens are full of tools that we use to cook and prepare our food. Even the smallest kitchen now has more tools and parts than the most wonderful kitchen in the world seven thousand years ago.

As people learned to use more and more plants for food, they also learned more ways to cook the plants and make them good to eat. Kitchens are usually very important for people. In a Hindu home in India, the kitchen is one of the sunniest, nicest rooms in the house. A lot of people like to sit and talk in their kitchen rather than in their living room.

Kitchen Gods

In ancient China the people believed that the god of every home lived in the hearth, or the fireplace, where the family did their cooking. Every Chinese home had a special niche in a wall near the hearth to hold a statue of the kitchen god.

This Spirit of the Hearth was honored once a year with a special day. The kitchen was cleaned and gifts of food on small plates were left by the hearth and around the niche for the god. This Spirit of the Hearth was very important because every year it reported to heaven all the bad deeds of every member of the family. Children were careful to speak quietly and kindly when they were near the hearth so that the Hearth Spirit would love them and give a good report on their behavior.

Seed Store

You have a store right in your own home where you can get seeds for a garden. This store is your kitchen.

Cut the green, leafy top off a carrot plant, leaving about a half-inch of orange root attached. Set the root in a shallow dish and keep the dish full of water.

If there is a tomato in your salad, pick out some yellow seeds and put them on a paper towel. Let them dry for a week and then plant them in a little pot. Keep the soil moist and see if they grow.

If you have oranges, lemons, or grapefruits in your refrigerator, plant the seeds from any of these fruits in a pot and let them grow.

Look for a sweet potato. Put one end of it in a small jar of water so that half of the potato is in the water. A long vine will slowly grow for you.

THE SECOND WEEK

MOON STORIES
A Story From Uganda

nce upon a time, many years ago, the sun and the moon could talk together. While talking one day, they decided that both of them had too many children. The sun and the moon agreed to kill their own children and make more room in the universe. The sun killed all his children, but the tenderhearted moon could not bear to kill one of his. So today the sun has no children, but the moon's children can be seen in the sky every night. They are the stars.

A Story From Papua

nce upon a time, a man dug a deep hole in the ground. Through the dirt he saw a bright light shining, so he dug and dug and uncovered a small, bright object. As he lifted the shining thing out of the hole, it grew larger and larger until it slipped from his hands and floated up into the sky where it could be seen shining in the night. It is the moon, and it would have been even brighter if the man had not dug it up but had let it be born out of the earth naturally.

A Story From Mozambique

nce upon a time, the moon was pale and did not shine. The sun was brilliant and bright, which made the moon jealous, so one day she stole some of the sun's fiery feathers for her own. The sun was angry. He wanted all the brightness of his feathers for himself. He found out who had taken some of his light and planned revenge. Picking up some mud, the sun splashed it over the moon and made dark spots that you can see today on the moon's face. The moon is still angry at the sun for throwing mud at her. Sometimes she surprises the sun and throws mud back at him.

MOON PLANTING

There are many stories and legends about the moon, how it got up in the sky and what it does. Before people had calendars, farmers could tell when to plant their seeds by counting the number of times that the moon had waxed or waned. However, most farmers and gardeners don't believe in this method of planting anymore.

People knew that the moon had a strong effect on the earth. The moon's revolution around the earth caused the tides to rise and fall in the ocean. As the moon grows from new moon to full moon, water that is deep under the earth rises. This water is called the water table, and farmers used the moon to tell them when to plant because of this action of the moon on the underground water.

Plants that needed a lot of water early in the stages of germination were planted when the moon was growing larger, or waxing. Farmers planted all the plants like lettuce and spinach, plants that grow above the ground, when the moon waxed.

Plants that didn't need so much water when they were planted were planted when the moon was getting smaller, or waning. Plants that grow under the ground like potatoes, carrots, and turnips were planted when the moon waned.

If you want to plant by the moon, here is when you plant.

The first quarter of the moon is best for planting leafy crops like lettuce.

The second quarter is best for plants that grow their seeds *inside* their fruit. Plants like squash, tomatoes, pumpkins, beans, and peas are planted during the second quarter.

The third quarter is the best time to plant things that grow for years, like trees, and root crops like onions, potatoes, radishes, and carrots.

The fourth quarter is not a good time for planting if you are planting by the moon.

You could try planting lettuce seed during all four quarters of the moon, once a week for four weeks. Then you can test the ancient way of planting seeds.

YOUR MOON

A lunar month is twenty-nine and one-half days long.
This is the time it takes the moon to go from a complete
full moon, when you can see the entire face of the moon
in a full circle, to the next full moon.

If you keep a chart of the moon's phases, you can
plant your garden the way the ancient farmers did.
Draw twenty-nine circles on a piece of paper or in your
journal to represent the face of the moon. Look at the
moon every night, and then draw the moon you see onto
one of the circles. Write the date under the moon you
have made and watch the moon change.

Do you know what makes the moon change its shape?
You can get a book from the library that explains why
the moon changes. Some Indians believed that there was
a fox in the sky who ate the moon every month and then
when it grew back, the fox would eat it again.

The Unhappy Mother—A Greek Myth

nce the world had no seasons. There was warm weather all twelve months of the year. This year-long summer was given to the world by Demeter. She was the goddess of agriculture and ruled over all the harvests and crops, the animals and food that men and women raised. Demeter had a daughter named Persephone, and she loved her daughter more than anything in the world.

Persephone was a beautiful girl, and she liked flowers. One day, she saw some particularly beautiful flowers. Persephone wandered farther and farther into a secluded valley, picking the soft-stemmed pink and yellow flowers until her skirt was full.

Suddenly the girl saw the ground in front of her split open, and a man driving eight black horses burst out of the earth. The terrified girl cried out as she dropped the flowers around her bare feet, and then shrieked in terror as the man picked her up and carried her in his iron chariot down into the very heart of the dark earth. As the ground closed over the chariot, Persephone cried loudly for her mother.

Demeter heard the cry that her daughter gave and looked for her all over the world, but Persephone was not to be found. Angry and frightened, Demeter ran from the mountains to the sea, ran through fields of grain, past flocks of goats and sheep, and hunted out the darkest parts of forests searching for her daughter, Persephone.

Finally Demeter went up in the blue heavens to the Sun himself, who sees all things on the earth, and begged him to tell her what had happened to her beloved daughter. The Sun, his great face burning with pity for Demeter, told her this story:

"Oh Demeter, your daughter lives now in the dark Underworld and is the Queen of that land. Hades, King of the Underworld, saw fair Persephone wandering among the flowers and fell in love with her. So in love was he, that he carried her away suddenly to be his bride. Nevermore can she return to earth and run through the fields at your side."

Demeter returned to the earth and wandered over the land, blind in her grief. She did not give rain to the earth nor did she help the new seeds to grow. She forgot the goats and sheep and neglected the grape vines.

The people of the villages were frightened. Their crops died in the fields and the grapes withered on the vines. The animals were sick.

The goats gave no milk for the children. The world was cold and sad. The men and women begged Zeus, King of the gods, to give Persephone back to her mother so that Demeter would once again bless their crops and make the land fruitful.

Zeus took pity on the farms and gardens of the people and agreed that Persephone must be returned to her mother, but only if the girl had eaten *nothing* while in the Underworld.

Poor Persephone! Wandering in Hades dark gardens, she had picked a pomegranate from a tree. Tearing open the leathery red rind, the girl had eaten seven of the pomegranate's juicy seeds.

Zeus heard this and was sad at first. Now Persephone could never return to her mother. But then he had an idea.

"Persephone must stay in the Underworld for seven months of every year, one month for each seed she has swallowed. The other five months of the year, Hades must return Persephone to her mother," Zeus said.

And this is why we have summer for five months of the year, while Persephone is with her mother and Demeter smiles upon the plants and animals. Then Persephone must return to her dark, underground kingdom and once again be Hades' queen for seven months. During these months, Demeter grieves, and the earth gradually becomes cold and barren. As

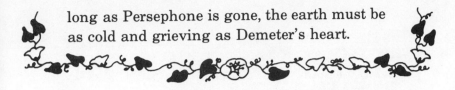

long as Persephone is gone, the earth must be as cold and grieving as Demeter's heart.

WEATHER

"The Unhappy Mother" is a story with which the ancient Greeks tried to explain why we have hot weather and cold weather, why the seasons come every year. Since people began, the weather has been very important for them. If it is too hot and dry, food is difficult to grow. When it rains for weeks and there are floods, the plants are washed away and die.

The earth has to be warm and moist for a seed to grow. Take some bean seeds and put them in a jar with a little water. Put the jar in the refrigerator. Look every week and see if the beans grow. Keep them damp, but don't let them get warm. What happens?

PLANTING

Every part of the world except for the very coldest Arctic lands and the driest deserts have a certain time of year when seeds can be planted outside and grow. If you live in warm Alabama, you can plant your seeds much earlier than if you live in colder Michigan. You wouldn't plant peas in Texas and Idaho on the same day because Idaho is much colder for most of the year than Texas is.

Look at the map on the next page. It is a map of the United States that has been divided up into different sections. Each section has a number.

Look at the numbers under the map and find the

1. May 20 to June 30
2. April 20 to May 20
3. March 30 to April 20
4. February 28 to March 30
5. January 1 to February 28

42 / February

number of the section where you live. Now you know when it is warm enough to plant seeds in your part of the country. This tells you the month when you can begin your garden outside.

THE FOURTH WEEK

ONION PRINTS

A bulb is a mass of fleshy leaves that overlap each other tightly to make a hard ball. In the center of the bulb is a bud that can grow into a plant.

Take two large yellow onions. Begin peeling the white onion leaves back, and you will see how they overlap. Onions make you cry before you can eat them.

Cut the other onion in half and look at the circles of leaves that protect the bud. You can make prints with the onion halves by dipping the cut side in ink or watercolor paint and then pressing the onion several times onto a piece of paper.

INDOOR GARDEN

Bulbs are usually planted outdoors in September, but you can plant them now and have a bowl of spring flowers for your family.

Buy some narcissus bulbs at your garden supply store. Take a clear glass bowl like an old fish bowl or several old jars that are about four or five inches deep. Put a shallow layer of well-washed charcoal (like the kind you use in aquarium filters) on the bottom of the container. Add an inch of pebbles or clear, glass marbles. The marbles are more fun because they let you see the roots growing.

Put the bulbs on top of the marbles so that the bulbs almost touch each other. Put more marbles in until the bulbs are half covered. Pour water very gently over the bulbs so they don't fall over. Fill the container only as high as the base of the bulbs. Do not cover the bulbs with water.

Put the planted bowl in a dark cool place, like your basement or the floor of a cool closet. Keep the bulbs in the dark and continue to add water each day so they don't dry out. Keep the water level up to the bottom of the bulbs.

When the bowl is full of roots and the bulbs are sprouting out the top, bring the bowl out into the light. Don't put it directly in the sun at first. Let the plants get used to the light gradually or they will get sunburned. Keep adding water so the roots will stay wet.

MARCH

For, lo, the winter
  is past,
The rain is over
  and gone;
The flowers appear
  on the earth;
The time of the
  singing of birds
  is come,
And the voice of
  the turtle is
  heard in our land.

—The Book of
Solomon

MARCH

THE FIRST WEEK

SEASON OF THE SENSES

March is still a cold month in part of our country, but most of the land is waking up and getting ready for summer. Go outside and look at the trees that you first looked at in January. Look closely at their branches and the tips of the branches to see if they look different. Watch the earth for signs of new plants, grass, or flowers.

Springtime is a season of the senses. You can smell and hear and see new things almost every day. There comes a day in spring when the earth has thawed enough, and you can smell the soil and all the growing things again. Smelling a hyacinth in springtime on a cool morning is enough to make the whole day seem happier.

Flocks of birds fly north during the spring to return to their nesting areas. You may see hundreds of robins or finches or ducks in a week if you look for them.

I was on a beach in California when a huge flock of sea birds landed one spring day. For an hour I walked on the beach, and the birds would separate for me, leaving a brown path among their whiteness. When they finally took off and flew away, the beach wasn't light brown anymore. It was covered with white feathers that moved over the sand like seafoam when the wind blew.

SPRING FEASTING

Some people used to eat eggs in the springtime and give colored eggs to friends as a present. The eggs symbolized new life and the beginnings of birth.

My great-grandmother liked to give all of us children peppermint tea as a spring tonic. She said that the peppermint would wake us up and get us ready to run outside all summer. Here is her recipe:

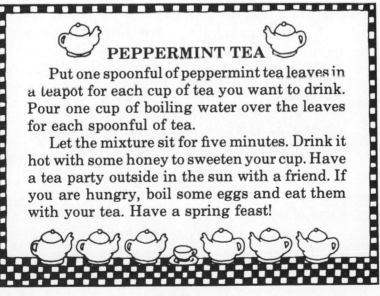

PEPPERMINT TEA

Put one spoonful of peppermint tea leaves in a teapot for each cup of tea you want to drink. Pour one cup of boiling water over the leaves for each spoonful of tea.

Let the mixture sit for five minutes. Drink it hot with some honey to sweeten your cup. Have a tea party outside in the sun with a friend. If you are hungry, boil some eggs and eat them with your tea. Have a spring feast!

THE SECOND WEEK

How the Earth Began—
A North American Indian Legend

There was once a great flood in the world. Water covered all the fields, the valleys, and even the tops of all the mountains. There was so much water that the animals were afraid that the earth was gone, and they would all die.

Floating on the water were logs and trees that had been pulled out of the earth by the flood water, and the animals clung to the branches during night and by day in the hope that the water would go away.

Floating on one large tree trunk was a turtle, a muskrat, a loon, and Coyote Man, the magical creature who lived in the southwestern part of the country.

Now Coyote Man was tired of being on the log. He turned the turtle upside down, pulled the muskrat's tail, and wouldn't let the loon have a minute's sleep, but these tricks began to bore him after a while, and Coyote Man wanted a dry place to lay his head for the next night.

"Go down to the bottom of the water," Coyote Man demanded of the turtle, "and bring me up a piece of mud." But the turtle refused. He was angry with Coyote Man for flipping him over on his back so many times.

So Coyote Man said to the loon, "Go down to the bottom of the water and bring me up a piece of mud." But the loon hadn't slept for a week, and she was too tired to swim so far.

Coyote Man looked at the muskrat. The muskrat had nothing left of his tail but a little stub because Coyote Man had been pulling it for a week.

"Please, muskrat," Coyote Man said, "go down to the bottom of the water and bring me up a piece of mud or we will all die."

The muskrat's tail was sore, but he didn't want to die, so he decided to trust Coyote Man. Diving into the water, the muskrat swam down out of the pale yellow water where the sun still could be seen, through the dark green water, down until he couldn't see any light at all, just cold, black water in his eyes.

For three days and three nights, Coyote Man waited for the muskrat on the cold, soaked tree trunk. Finally the muskrat came swimming up out of the water.

Crawling up on the tree trunk, the muskrat was so waterlogged that he was nearly dead. He rolled over on his back and just lay there, but in one tightly clasped paw there was a single lump of mud.

Coyote Man grabbed this lump and, reciting magic charms, placed the mud on the surface of the water. There it floated, and for four days and nights the lump of dirt got bigger and bigger until it made valleys and fields and even the mountains—the earth as we know it. All the animals and Coyote Man stepped ashore and life began again.

COMPOST—AND HOW TO MAKE IT

It would be impossible to create earth the way Coyote Man did, but you can make compost instead, without the need to recite magic words. Compost is a mixture of vegetable scraps from your kitchen, together with dirt, sand, leaves, sawdust, manure, small sticks, and just about anything else you want to add. Farmers and gardeners build compost piles outside and use up all their kitchen scraps, weeds, animal manure, and leaves. When the minerals in these things are put back into the soil the dirt is enriched and you will be able to grow healthy plants. Good gardeners never have to waste anything if they have a compost pile.

As all the things mix together in a compost pile, air, water, earthworms, and bacteria break up the leaves and sticks and kitchen scraps. After a while you have a rich, dark, crumbly mixture. Plants *love* it. A gardener can never have too much compost.

Take an old garbage can, pail, or heavy plastic sack. Put some dirt in it from the garden. Then add leaves, vegetable scraps from the kitchen (carrot tops, onion skins, celery tops, potato peels) weeds, some manure if you have it.

Stir it up and pour a cup or two of water over it to make it just barely damp if the dirt isn't damp already. Don't let it get so wet that it is soggy. You can put the can out in the yard and keep adding things to it. If it smells, put more dirt and leaves in. By the time your garden is ready to be planted, you will have rich compost to add to the soil.

If you live in an apartment, mix dirt and chopped vegetable scraps together in a coffee can. Keep a tight lid on the can, but open it up and stir it once a day. Add a little water, but only to moisten. If it gets too soggy, dump half out and add more dirt. When it is all crumbly, you can use it in your potting containers indoors.

THE THIRD WEEK

FORAGING

Foraging means to roam around looking for things that are useful to you. It doesn't mean going to a store and looking for something to buy but rather, finding things that no one else wants and using them.

If you are going to have a garden, foraging is useful. Weeds, grass clippings, and leaves are all good for the soil in your garden. When your neighbors mow their lawns, you can ask them if you can rake up the clipped grass. It is good to spread around your plants because it has lots of minerals like phosphorous, nitrogen, potassium, calcium, and iron. When you grow vegetables in mineral-rich soil, you get super vegetables!

Keep your eyes open when you are on hikes too. You may see interesting rocks that you could use to put around the edges of your garden after it is planted. If you walk through the woods, you may find enough dead sticks on the ground to make a fence for your garden. A string and stick fence will keep dogs out.

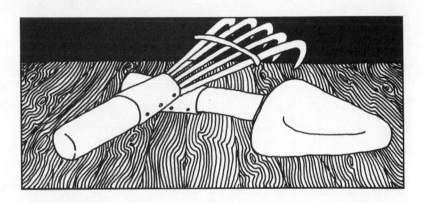

Sometimes people throw out their old garden tools when they buy new ones. Ask if you can have the old tools or look to make up your own. I once knew a lady who gardened all summer with only an old dinner fork for a tool.

TREES

The trees in March are usually putting out new leaves every day. This is a good time to start a leaf collection. Pick a leaf from every tree in your neighborhood. Be sure and ask permission if the trees are in someone else's yard. If you live in a city, go to a park and collect leaves there.

Put each leaf between two sheets of wax paper and put the paper and leaves between the pages of a large book. The book will hold the leaf flat while it dries so that it won't curl up.

white oak

ginko

elm

sweet gum

Go to the library and get a book with pictures of trees and their leaves. See how many of your leaves you can name. When the leaves are dry, you can tape them in a scrapbook or on paper and have a book of your own. If you are keeping a journal, it could hold your leaf collection.

A Contest—A Greek Myth

Once upon a time there was a lovely young girl who wove the most beautiful cloth in all the world. Her name was Arachne, and she was very proud of her talent.

People came from all the villages to see Arachne weave her cloth. Arachne grew so proud that she challenged Athene herself, the goddess of weaving, to a contest.

Athene was angry at Arachne's great pride and accepted the girl's challenge. Setting her loom up by the girl's, Athene wove for three days and three nights. She wove scenes of the gods' and goddesses' great heroic deeds.

Then Arachne set up her loom and also wove for three days and three nights. The girl wove beautiful pictures showing all the silly and evil deeds of the gods and goddesses.

When they were both done, everyone agreed that Arachne's cloth was more beautiful than the cloth woven by the goddess.

Athene was so angry that she swelled with rage. In her temper she broke to pieces Arachne's loom and weaving tools. Then the goddess destroyed all the beautiful, glittering cloth that the girl had woven.

Poor Arachne! She was so unhappy and distraught that she hanged herself.

When Athene heard that the girl was dead, she was ashamed and returned to earth with tears falling over her bright face. Picking up Arachne's body in her arms, Athene changed the girl into an eight-legged insect.

"You will live forever as a spider," said Athene. "Now you will weave your gossamer cloth all over the world, and people will say that you are the most skillful weaver on earth."

SPIDER ART

There are certainly a lot of spiders in the world. In a single one-acre field in England, there are about two and a quarter million spiders. They help the gardeners because spiders eat other insects. In England and Wales alone (look for those countries on a globe or in an atlas of the world), spiders kill 200 trillion insects a year. Don't ever kill the spiders in your garden. They are helping you.

You can collect spider webs. Get some dark construction paper, black or dark blue, red, or green, and a can of white spray paint. Go out in the woods, in your yard or in a park and look for a beautiful spider's web. Chase the spider away gently with a piece of grass so it won't be killed by the paint. Then spray the web lightly until it is all white. Get a friend to hold a piece of construction paper under the web while you break the connecting strands gently. The web will stick to the paper. When it is dry, you can hang it up on your wall. You will have a picture that a spider made—spider art.

THE FOURTH WEEK

TIME TO BEGIN

Most of the country has warmed up since January. The ground is getting soft and warm. It is time to plan where your vegetables and flowers should be planted. Maybe there isn't much planning involved. There is only one part of my backyard that has enough sun and space for a garden. Perhaps you already know where you can have a garden.

Look for these things for your garden. There should be lots of sun—the more sun, the better, so stay away from trees if you can. Don't plant your garden where people will walk on it. Put it in a safe spot. It should be within easy reach of a hose so you can water the plants if they need it. Make sure that it is all right with your family for you to have a garden there.

If you live in an apartment in the city, you have to be more resourceful. Get an adult or big brother or sister to help you build shelves by a sunny window. Maybe you can find a cheap table at a sale or junk shop to hold your plants. Pick the sunniest window you have.

If there isn't much sun in your apartment, maybe your city has public parks where people can have garden plots. Call up your city's park service and ask them. Maybe you have a neighbor or a friend who has a sunny window that you can use.

They are rather expensive, but there are special lights for growing plants that you can buy in a hardware store. Ask your family and see what they suggest.

Digging

If your garden is outside, the first job is to dig it up. Use a large garden fork or shovel and try to turn the soil over as deep as it is possible to get the fork in. Have someone help you with this first part if you can't do it. Don't try to do it too fast. You can work on it for a week.

Then you can take a small garden fork, trowel, or an old kitchen fork and break the lumps of dirt up. Start at one corner and work down. Don't walk on the dirt after it is broken up. You will pack it down and squeeze all the air out of it. Plant roots like air. You do not want the soil to be hard and mashed down.

After the ground is broken up, you can spread leaves, grass clippings, finely chopped weeds, or hay over the ground. They will be good for the soil and help the new seedlings when you plant them.

You can even name your garden. Lots of famous gardens have names. The Hanging Gardens of ancient Babylon and the Garden of Eden both had names. Your garden can have a name too.

APRIL

Pippa's Song

The year's at the spring
And the day's at the
  morn;
Morning's at seven;
The hillside's dew-
  pearled;
The lark's on the wing;
The snail's on the thorn:
God's in his heaven—
All's right with the
  world!

      —Robert Browning

Peas

onions

APRIL

THE FIRST WEEK

PLANNING YOUR GARDEN

Now it is time to plan your garden. Here is a way to do it. Measure your garden carefully. Then draw a picture of it. You can use one or two inches on paper for every foot of garden you have. A garden that is six feet by four feet would be six inches by four inches on paper.

Now you can see exactly how much space you have. A garden that is small won't hold as much as a larger garden, but it won't be as much work. If you have as much as six feet by four feet, you will have enough room for:

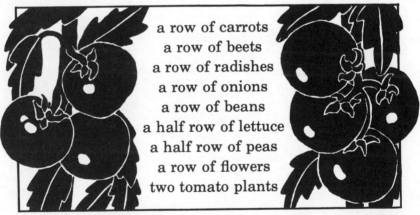

a row of carrots
a row of beets
a row of radishes
a row of onions
a row of beans
a half row of lettuce
a half row of peas
a row of flowers
two tomato plants

If you want to grow pumpkins, squash, or watermelons, you will need a special space just for them because they spread out and take up more room. If you grow corn, it must be planted in a block at least four feet by three feet so that it can be pollinated.

Plants make their seeds and fruit by reproduction. To reproduce, the plants must be fertilized. This is done with pollen and eggs. Plants produce pollen, which is the dusty, yellow stuff that you see in the center of many flowers. Pollen is the plant's sperm, the male part of the plant. It must be carried by the wind or by bees and insects to the female part of the flower, the pistil, where the plant's eggs are found. When corn is planted closely together in one solid patch, more of the plants will be fertilized because the pollen will blow over all the plants. One lonely corn stalk will have less chance of getting enough pollen to produce ears of corn.

Plants like green beans, peas, and cucumbers can be planted around three sticks stuck in the ground and tied at the top to look like a tripod. Then they take up less room.

Flowers can have their own part in your garden or they can be mixed in with the vegetables.

If you buy onion sets (small onions ready to plant from the nursery), a garlic bulb, and marigolds, you can fight off some bugs. A row of these plants will keep the other vegetables safer from bugs because some bugs don't like the smell of onions, garlic, and marigolds.

Lists

Make a drawing of your garden.

Then make a list under it of your favorite vegetables and flowers.

If you want some ideas, go to a seed store or nursery and look at the packages of seeds.

THE SECOND WEEK

PLANTING

By this time of year, vegetables can be planted in most parts of the country. The first things you plant should be vegetables that do well in spring weather. You can ask at your local nursery and find out which vegetables can be planted first in your area. Look on the back of seed packages, too. They will often tell you when you can plant the vegetable.

You could start planting by working on the soil in your garden where the first row will go. Break up all the large sods of dirt. Crumble the dirt in your hands and chop it up. Make it fine and even and loose for the seeds.

ONIONS

People have been eating onions for thousands of years. The ancient Egyptians used onions. People in China and India grew onions. The onion was loved for the good flavor it gave to meat and vegetable dishes. It was easy to store and didn't need to be kept in a cold place to be fresh, so people grew many kinds of onions and put them in cellars dug in the ground. All winter, people could use the onions when other vegetables were no longer available.

The best way to grow onions is from onion sets. These are small onions that you buy from a nursery. Each onion should be planted about two inches deep, about three or four inches from each other. Cover them up and pat the soil gently. The onion will grow a long, green top first. Then there is sometimes a beautiful, white flower. When the onion tops turn yellow and brown and fall over in three months, it is time to dig up the onions carefully from the ground. Brush the dirt off gently and let them sit all day in the sun to dry a little. Then they can be stored in a cool place, like your basement or garage.

The green onion tops can be snipped with scissors and used on top of baked potatoes with sour cream.

GARLIC

Garlic has been used to season food for so long that no one knows where it was first grown. It is one of the things that makes pizza and Italian spaghetti sauce taste so good.

In the Middle Ages, about a thousand years ago, until fairly recently, garlic was believed to be a strong medicine and cure for just about anything. People wore garlic on strings around their necks so they wouldn't catch colds, flu, and even the Black Death. Other folks said that chewing garlic all day kept them from getting sick. The garlic smell would certainly have kept most people away, and then the germs wouldn't be spread so quickly, but it was a hard way to stay well.

Often people were afraid to walk around at night for fear of vampires. It was said that vampires were afraid of garlic, so most people carried garlic when they went out at night. If you are afraid of the dark, you can do what children did hundreds of years ago and hang a bulb of garlic over your head to keep you safe. It may make you feel better.

You can plant garlic right next to onions. These plants like to grow next to each other.

Take a bulb of garlic. If you break it apart with your fingers, you will see that it is made up of small, waxy pieces called "cloves." Each clove should be planted separately about one or two inches deep, four inches from the next garlic clove or onion set. They will flower and then their green tops will yellow and wither. Then the tops can be braided together by the bulbs like a chain. You can hang your chain of garlic on the kitchen wall and use it all next winter.

The Princess and the Pea—A Fairy Tale

Once upon a time there was a Prince who was looking for a wife. Being a Prince, of course, he could only marry a Princess, but true Princesses were hard to find. The Prince sent out word to all the kingdoms around that he was looking for a Princess, and several months later, twelve young maidens rode up to the castle on twelve white mares.

The young maidens said that they were all Princesses, and the Prince might take his pick of them for a wife. All of the girls were equally beautiful and equally intelligent and well-mannered, so the young Prince could not decide which one to choose for his wife.

His mother, who was a wise old woman, suggested that the young women be the Prince's guests for a week. The girls agreed, and that night they each slept in lovely beds hung with silken draperies and golden cloth. Every night the Prince held a grand ball for the maidens and took turns dancing with each one of them.

Now the girls did not know it, but under the mattress of each lovely bed the wise Queen had placed a single, dried pea.

The first morning after the girls had slept in their beds, the Queen asked, "And how did you sleep last night, my dears?"

All the girls said that never had they slept so well in all their life, except for the youngest maiden. She hesitated, but then said softly, "My bed is very beautiful, your Majesty, but never have I slept so little in all my life."

The other maidens scolded the youngest girl for complaining, but the Queen smiled and ordered the servants to put another mattress on the youngest girl's bed.

And every morning for seven days it was again like that. Eleven of the maidens rose from their beds radiant and rested, but the youngest girl grew pale and tired, for she could not sleep.

In a week the Queen sent the oldest eleven girls home on their eleven white mares and presented the youngest maiden to her son.

"This is your bride, my son," she said. "She is a true Princess, for even through seven mattresses she could feel the harsh lump of a single dried pea under her delicate body."

The Prince rejoiced to have found a true Princess and they were married the next day with joy and feasting.

PEAS

Peas are a very ancient food. They are delicious when eaten fresh off the vines, and they are easy to dry. When people dried peas and stored them in sacks, they had an excellent food for the long winters when they couldn't grow any fresh vegetables.

This week you can plant peas. Buy a package of seed at your supermarket or nursery. Bush peas grow lower to the ground and are easier to pick. They are a better choice for a small garden than peas that are climbing-type peas.

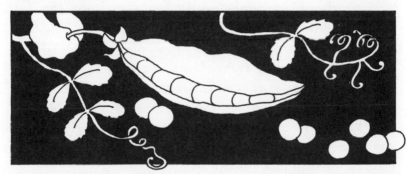

Make a line in the soil about a foot behind your onion row. Make this furrow an inch deep. Lay the pea seeds one or two inches apart in the furrow and then cover them up with crumbly dirt. Pat them down gently.

As the pea bushes grow larger and heavier with the pea pods, you may need to put two strong sticks at each end of the furrow. Tie wire on the sticks, and stretch the wire tightly from stick to stick across the row. Then you can tie the pea plants gently to the wire with string as they grow. This will hold the plants off the ground so that snails and bugs can't find the peas.

The peas are delicious raw when they are small and tender. Try snacking on them. You might like to plant some snow peas, or Chinese peas, as they are called. You can eat the pods of these peas as well as the seeds inside.

CARROTS

If you had given a bouquet of flowers to someone a thousand years ago, you would have used carrot tops as part of the bouquet. Their feathery green foliage were much admired then and were used with flowers as decoration.

Carrots are not only pretty but very good for you. They are full of vitamin A and other vitamins. They are also easy to grow.

Buy a package of carrot seed and pour half the seeds into a small paper cup. Add a few spoonfuls of dry sand to the seeds in the cup and put the rest of the seed away. The sand will help you handle these tiny seeds more easily. You can use the other half of the seed for a second crop of carrots later in the summer.

Make sure your dirt is very well dug and loose. Carrots like to push down in the earth, and they can't grow if the ground is too hard.

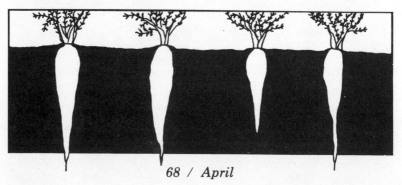

Draw another furrow in the dirt and plant the seeds mixed with sand, sprinkling them evenly down the furrow. You can plant the carrots four or five inches from your row of peas.

If you are losing track of your rows, put a stick in the ground at the end of each row and tie thread to the sticks. Draw a picture of a carrot and a pea or use the seed package to mark where the vegetables are planted. If birds are scratching around trying to find your peas, tie four or five black threads to sticks in a crisscross over the rows. The birds will fly down for a snack, not see the black thread and bump into it. This will scare them away.

Lightly water the soil over the peas and carrots and keep it damp so the seeds can germinate, or sprout. Don't get it too wet or you will wash away the seeds.

THE FOURTH WEEK

SPRING FUN

In a few days it will be the first day of May. The first of May, or May Day, has been celebrated for centuries as an important time of year for gardeners and farmers.

May marked the beginning of warm weather in many countries, and people celebrated by trying to bring good luck to the harvest.

Women, men, and children went out early in the morning on May Day and cut down green branches, picked flowers, cut small trees and decorated them with

April / 69

ribbons and cloth. They danced and sang around the tree with wreaths of flowers on their heads. In some countries a green bush was placed at the door of every house and garlands of flowers and greenery decorated the walls and windows of every cottage. Everyone celebrated the return of warm weather and prayed that the newly sown seeds would bring in a good harvest.

May Baskets

One custom that we have from these ancient times is making May baskets. Cut baskets out of brightly colored construction paper following the pattern on the next page or make up your own design for a May basket.

Get up very early on May first and fill the baskets with leaves, grass, green plants, and any flowers you can find. Dandelions and violets are nice to use, and so is clover.

Put May baskets on your neighbors' porches or by their doors if you live in an apartment. Let them celebrate the coming of summer and your new garden on this first day of May just as people have done for thousands of years.

Have a warm and happy May Day.

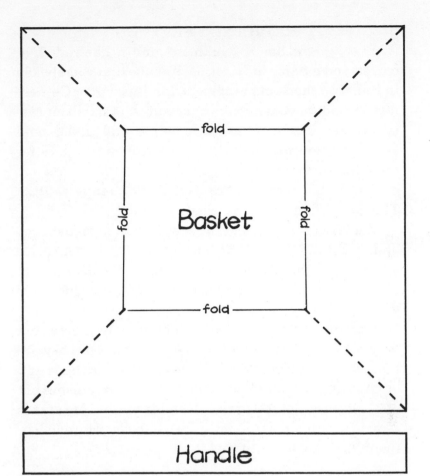

Cut a square out of paper this size—or larger, to make a bigger basket. Cut in from each corner as shown by dotted lines, making all cuts the same length. Fold each side up where fold lines are shown, then tape or glue overlapping points to form basket walls. Cut out a strip of paper for handle, then tape or glue across middle of basket.

April / 71

RAPHANUS SATIVUS

Every plant has a "common" name, like radish or carrot, and a name in Latin, a language that was spoken in Italy two thousand years ago. If a Russian or Chinese farmer and an American farmer want to talk about radishes, they can use the Latin name and understand each other even though they know different names for the plant in their own language.

The Latin name for "radish" is *Raphanus sativus*. This Latin name means "easily grown."

Radishes are very easy to grow. Buy some radish seed and sow it in a line about four inches from your carrot seeds. Make the furrow about one-half inch deep, sprinkle the seed in, and crumble dirt over it. Pat the top of your radish row gently.

Radishes are not only beautiful and easy to grow, but they also have a lot of vitamin C in them too. They are best when they aren't too old. Old radishes are huge and often very hot. I once knew a boy who loved radishes but didn't like the hot feel of radish on his tongue. He ate his radishes with a glass of milk and dipped each radish in the milk as he ate it to cool it off!

MAY

And I bowed my body
  and beheld all about
And saw the sun and
  the sea and the
  sand after,
And where the birds
  and beasts walked
  by their mates,
Wild wormes in woods
  and wonderful
  fowls
With flecked feathers
  and many colors.

—William Langland
  about 1370

MAY

THE FIRST WEEK

The Silly Woman—A Cochiti Indian Story

Many moons ago there lived a woman named Yellow Woman. She had a large field of squash and worked every day in the hot sun weeding and caring for her plants.

One day, while Yellow Woman was working in her field, she heard a locust singing in the bushes by the squash plants.

Yellow Woman was pleased by the song of the locust and called out, "Please locust, sing your song again for me."

But the locust was very shrewd. "I won't sing again unless you give me something," said the insect.

Yellow Woman thought hard. What could she give the locust?

"There is nothing I own that you would want, locust, except this field of squash," she called out. "I will give you and your children and grandchildren all the squash that they can eat if you will just sing your song for me."

The locust agreed to Yellow Woman's offer

and sang sweetly all afternoon, but Yellow Woman's mother and father were not so pleased. "Stupid girl!" they cried. "You have given our food away to the locusts." The parents were so angry that they drove Yellow Woman away from her home.

And so it has been ever since. The locusts appear wherever squash are planted, and they know that it is their right to feast on the yellow fruit of the squash plant.

SQUASH

Squash are plants that first grew in North, Central, and South America. People in Europe only grew squash after Columbus and other explorers brought back seeds from the new land.

Squash, fresh and dried, was one of the main foods of people in the Southwest of our country. The squash was a sacred plant for many Indian tribes. Like corn and tomatoes, squash is one of the foods that we have to thank the Indians for giving us.

The Huichol Indians made a six day trip every year from their home in Mexico to the Pacific Ocean. When they reached the Pacific beaches, they filled several gourds of sea water, which they carried home and used for religious ceremonies. Since they were taking sea water away from the ocean, the Indians gave the sea gods a present in return. It was the most precious gift they could give, bowls of squash seeds, which they flung into the water.

Growing a Squash

You may have room for a squash plant in your garden. Each plant will take up a piece of ground about three feet by three feet. If your garden is too small, see if you can find an old planter box, a barrel, or an old garbage pail. You could fill the container with dirt and compost or manure, and grow a squash outside your garden.

If you live in an apartment, you will have trouble growing such a large plant unless you have a very big space. Even then, it will be hard for the squash plant to be fertilized inside with no bees to help pollinate the plant. Don't worry. Other plants like lettuces, carrots, radishes, and herbs are perfect for indoors.

What Kind?

There are many types of squash that you can grow. You can go to a nursery and look at the seed packages and decide which kind you like best.

Acorn squash takes a long time to grow. The quickest and easiest squashes to grow are zucchini and yellow squash. Do you have room for one or two squash plants in your garden?

If so, plant them like this. Dig a hole about a foot across and six inches deep, at least three feet from the other rows you have planted. Put some compost or manure in the hole. Pile the dirt up on top of the manure and make a hill. Hollow the top of the hill a little and drop in three or four squash seeds. Cover them up with an inch or two of dirt. Keep the hill damp but don't wash it away. When the seedlings come up, pull out the weakest-looking ones and leave the strongest two.

If you plant a zucchini plant, you will be surprised at how fast the green zucchini can grow. They can grow two feet long in a week, it seems. The zucchini are best if you pick them when they are small, about six inches long, but you can let one zucchini grow until it won't grow anymore.

If you have a friend or a sister or brother with a garden, you could share seeds with them. Then you might have a contest to see who can grow the largest zucchini.

THE SECOND WEEK

TOMATOES

Tomatoes were first grown in the Andes Mountains of Peru. When they were brought to Europe, the plant was grown for decoration, but no one ate the fruit. Until about 1812, European people believed that tomatoes were poisonous. The tomato is a cousin of the deadly nightshade, a very poisonous plant, and Europeans thought that tomatoes would kill them if they ate them. Even a hundred years ago, some people still believed that tomatoes were poisonous. Thomas Jefferson was probably the first person to grow tomatoes in our country who wasn't an Indian.

The Indians were right. Tomatoes are safe, delicious, and one of the best plants you can grow. They are actually a fruit and have lots of vitamins A, B, and C in them. When you eat a bacon, lettuce, and tomato sandwich, you can thank the Indians for your lunch.

Growing Tomatoes

Tomatoes are easy to grow. There are many different kinds of tomatoes. The nice thing about growing your own is that you don't have to worry about shipping the tomatoes in boxes all over the country the way farmers do. You can grow tomatoes with thin, tender skins that wouldn't ship well. They are usually better than the tomatoes you get in stores. You can also let your tomatoes get ripe right on the plant. Farmers can't do this.

Farmers pick their tomatoes while they are still green. They put them in crates and put the crates in a room. Then they fill the room with a gas that helps the tomatoes turn red even though they aren't on the vine anymore. Tomatoes in stores are bright red and look just like the ones in your garden, but the ones from your garden will taste better.

Dig some manure or compost into your dirt and plant seed in two or three clumps about two and a half feet apart.

When the tomato seeds come up, pull out all the seedlings, leaving one every two and a half feet. One or two tomato plants will give you lots of tomato soup.

Tomatoes all need some poles in back of them to tie the side branches onto. If the plant lies on the ground, the worms and bugs will get all your tomatoes before you can get them yourself.

Sometimes it is hard to grow tomatoes indoors, but you might like to try if you live in an apartment. It will make a lovely, green plant even if you don't get much fruit. Add a little fertilizer to your tomato plant each week. Putting just a little in each week is better than throwing a whole lot in every three weeks. Don't over-water your tomato plant. You could try cherry tomato plants. They are nice, bite-size tomatoes for salads and snacks.

LETTUCE

Nearly everybody loves salad. Twenty-five hundred years ago, lettuce was grown in the royal gardens of Persia. It was grown and loved in China. The Romans ate salad every day. The English and Italians loved let-

tuce. A crunchy leaf of lettuce picked fresh and washed off with a hose is one of the world's nicest snacks.

Pick out a package of lettuce seeds. Make the soil very crumbly and fine. You can plant a row or just throw the seed down on fine soil in a little area. Cover it with enough dirt so there is about a quarter of an inch of dirt over the seed. Pat it down gently. Keep it moist and water it often. Lettuce likes moisture.

If you live in an apartment, lettuce is perfect for you to grow. It looks just beautiful grown in a line of pots in a window. You can have a whole salad in one window, with an onion or two, lettuce, radishes, and some pots of herbs like marjoram and basil to put in the salad dressing!

THE DREAD SNAIL

When you have all these lettuce, pea, and squash seedlings coming up in your garden, you will also have snails. Every year I fight a battle with snails. My backyard seems to produce more snails than anything else I grow. Some days I feel like calling my whole backyard "The Snail Farm."

I must admit, though, that snails are interesting. Go out early some morning and find a snail to watch or go to an aquarium or tropical fish store in your city and look at the water snails.

The scientific name of the snail is *gastropod*, which means "belly-foot." That is because the bottom of a snail that it uses to ooze along on acts like a foot, but it is *also* its stomach!

The snail has two tiny eyes on the end of its upper

tentacles and no nose at all. It breathes through tiny openings on the upper part of the foot (which is its body), near the shell.

The two lower tentacles and the skin of the snail are very sensitive and can feel vibrations, like the vibrations you make on the ground when you walk. The snail uses its skin and tentacles almost like you use your ears.

Try an experiment. Lie down on the ground and mash your ear against the earth. Have a friend walk firmly toward you from a distance. How close does your friend have to get before you can hear him? This is the way that Indians used to listen to the earth for the sound of buffalo hooves. If they heard vibrations, then the buffalo were near, maybe over the next hill. Try listening to the earth and see how good a snail you'd make.

Snails look really cute, but if you saw an enlarged picture of their mouth, you would see why gardeners *do not* love snails. The snail's tongue is like a ribbon covered with hundreds of tiny, hooked teeth. Some snails have over 27,000 teeth, and every snail in your backyard is going to try to get at your helpless seedlings.

Sometimes I plant a whole row of seeds and the green seedlings don't come up. Actually, they did come up, but the snails got the seedlings before I could get the snails.

There are several ways to kill snails. You can pour two or three inches of stale beer into cake pans and put them near your seedlings. The snails like the beer and they fall into the pans and drown. This works for some people. Most of the snails in my backyard just consider this an extra treat.

You can buy a bag of sand and put a path of sand all around your garden. Snails don't like to crawl over the sand. This is a pretty solution, but the sand gets ground into the dirt pretty quick.

One of the most fun and best ways to get rid of snails is to have a Great Snail Hunt. Get up very early in the morning or have the hunt after dark with flashlights if you like more of a challenge. Snails hide under rocks and bushes and come out when the sun isn't so hot.

Give each hunter a plastic sack and then let them comb the yard for the snails. Put all the snails in the sacks. When the hunt is over, tie the tops of the plastic sacks firmly and put them in the garbage can. Maybe you could offer a prize for the most snails caught.

THE THIRD WEEK

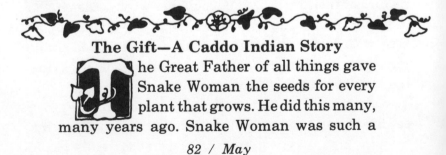

The Gift—A Caddo Indian Story

he Great Father of all things gave Snake Woman the seeds for every plant that grows. He did this many, many years ago. Snake Woman was such a good gardener that in a few years she had more seeds than she could plant by herself, so she and her two strong sons set out with the seeds on a journey. They gave the seeds to all the men and women they met and told them how to plant them for good harvests.

Snake Woman warned every woman and man who took the seeds that there were three rules for growing bean seeds. The people must plant the seeds correctly, care for the plants when they grew, and *never, never* let any child touch the bean plants.

The Caddo Indian people did as Snake Woman told them, and for this reason Caddo children were never allowed to work in the bean fields.

BEANS

Fortunately, most of us are not Caddo Indian children. We can grow beans and have beautiful, easy-to-grow bean plants in our gardens.

Beans come in many varieties. Snap beans or green beans grow on bushes or on long vines. The bushes are easier to care for. They are low and don't need stakes to grow on.

If you select seeds that are the climbing type of green beans, you can make a bean teepee. Put three long poles, about six feet tall, in the ground. Tie them at the top like a teepee.

Plant four to six bean seeds in a circle around the

bottom of each pole. As the bean plants grow, tie them onto the poles. Soon you will have a green, growing teepee. I had a teepee like this last summer, and my cat thought I had made it for her. She took naps in the teepee under the bean plants every hot afternoon.

Make sure the dirt is crumbly and plant your beans only a half-inch deep. They need good, regular watering, but don't overdo it. Bean plants don't like to sit in puddles.

CUCUMBERS

Cucumbers are a very ancient food. They were grown in India thousands of years ago and have been loved by Roman Emperors, French kings, and people like us for centuries.

If you want a couple of cucumber plants in your garden, try to find a small stepladder that has been thrown out or an old trellis. Cucumbers grow on a vine, and they take up less room when tied up off the ground. You can plant cucumbers on both sides of an old ladder or stake them like tomatoes with a stick and string.

Plant the cucumber seed only a half-inch deep and pick the cucumbers as soon as they are about four to six inches long. The plant will grow more cucumbers if you pick them regularly.

How'd You Do That?

Pick out one cucumber when it is only about an inch long and very thin. Leave it on the vine, but slip the baby cucumber gently into a bottle with a small neck. Cover the bottle with a newspaper so the sun doesn't shine through the glass and dry up the cucumber. When the cucumber is grown, cut the stem. Now you have a cucumber in a bottle, but the cuke won't come out the bottle's narrow neck. Your friends will ask, "How'd you do that?"

THE FOURTH WEEK

Clytie—A Greek Myth

Clytie was a water nymph who lived long, long ago. She loved her green world under the sea and played with her dear sisters all day, chasing each other through the forests of coral and shell deep beneath the waves.

One day, Clytie saw a bright golden light above her and, being curious, she swam up through the salty water to see what it was. Crawling out of the water onto a bank, she saw the beautiful god of the sun, Apollo, driving his flaming chariot across the sky.

Clytie fell in love with him. His golden splendor was so great that Clytie forgot her sisters and friends under the cool, green sea. She saw only Apollo.

For nine days and nine nights, Clytie sat on the bank and turned her face toward the sun god as he moved across the sky from east to west. In vain, her sisters begged Clytie to come back to her ocean home.

After nine days, Clytie was nearly dead from hunger. She was not used to the harsh, dry wind and the sun's glare.

The Goddess of Love, Aphrodite, saw Clytie and took pity on her. "Dear Clytie," said Aphrodite, "your constant and faithful love will be rewarded. Never again will you have to turn away from your love, the Sun, and your children will love him as constantly as you."

As the goddess spoke, Clytie's long hair turned into leaves, her feet grew rooted into the ground and her lovely face became golden and radiant as the sun itself. Some people say that Clytie turned into the variety of flower called the heliotrope (like the sunflower, or the marigold), her golden head faces the sun every day as long as he drives his fiery chariot across the sky.

CORN

It is not a good idea to plant one or two corn seeds by themselves. Corn plants have to be planted in patches about three feet by three feet or they can't germinate and make the ears of corn. If you have a large enough garden, you can plant corn seeds about two inches deep, five or six inches apart. Corn plants love water, so water the new seedlings regularly.

Birds are real corn lovers just like people. Corn is one

of their favorite foods. If you plant corn, put five or six sticks in the ground in your corn patch. Tie thin strips of cloth on the sticks so it will move in the wind. This may help keep birds away from the seed. If that doesn't work, put a clear plastic cup over each seed when you plant them. When the plant comes up, take the cups off.

Corn grows so fast in hot weather that you can hear it grow. That's true. Stand in a field of corn on a still, hot night and listen. Even when there is no wind, the whole field rustles and creaks because the corn is growing so fast that it is moving.

SUNFLOWERS

Sunflowers are great. They were used as ornaments and food by the Indians of Central America long before they were discovered by Europeans. The plants grow six to eight feet tall and have a gorgeous flower at the top. The center of this flower is a round, tightly packed mass of seeds. Dried, they make wonderful snacks, or you can put them in a bird feeder.

Maybe you can plant two sunflower seeds in your

garden. They are worth squeezing in at two corners. One can be for you, one for the birds.

Plant two or three sunflower seeds a few inches apart in two corners of your garden. The sunflower grows straight up, so it doesn't take much room. When the plant is tall, you may need to tie it to a stake so it doesn't get blown over.

If you want the birds to have the seeds, just let them help themselves. A sunflower is a ready-made bird feeder. If you want the seeds for yourself, put a light paper sack over the flower and tie it around the stem when the seeds are large enough to attract birds. Get someone to help you because you don't want to break the stem. Then, when the plant is older, cut the stem and hang the flower upside down in a closet or kitchen window to dry.

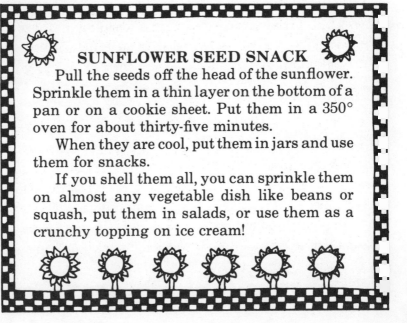

SUNFLOWER SEED SNACK

Pull the seeds off the head of the sunflower. Sprinkle them in a thin layer on the bottom of a pan or on a cookie sheet. Put them in a 350° oven for about thirty-five minutes.

When they are cool, put them in jars and use them for snacks.

If you shell them all, you can sprinkle them on almost any vegetable dish like beans or squash, put them in salads, or use them as a crunchy topping on ice cream!

JUNE
And what is so rare as a day in June? Then, if ever, come perfect days;

-James Russell Lowell
(1819-1881)

JUNE

THE FIRST WEEK

THE ALL-PURPOSE PLANTS

If you had lived five hundred years ago, it would have been difficult for you to get medicine when you were sick. When winter came and all the vegetables were gone, you would have had to think about what you could put in your bread and meat and oatmeal to make it taste more interesting. When it was freezing cold and you could not open any windows, you would have had to find some way to make your house smell better, and to get rid of your dog's fleas.

You would have used certain plants called herbs for all of these things, and we use herbs now. Look in the kitchen for spices. You should find small bottles or cans of dark green, dried leaves. Oregano, basil, thyme, and mint are all herbs. They are what make our food taste better.

Herbs are a little different from other plants. After the herb flowers, its stem dies. The stems of most herbs don't keep standing up like other plants after the flowering. The leaves, roots, and stems of herbs are used by people for a variety of purposes.

Nearly every plant and herb has been used at some time as a medicine. Sometimes the people were not right in thinking that the plant would help them prevent or cure sickness.

People ate parsley with their food. They often grew pots of parsley indoors and ate the herb all winter. Parsley is high in vitamin C and is good for you. Years ago, people didn't know about vitamins, but they knew that parsley made them feel better.

Tea made from tansy has been used for hundreds of years for stomach cramps. It wouldn't help you if you had appendicitis, but it might help a mild stomachache.

Herbs were used to season food years ago just as cooks use them today. Hundreds of years ago, no one understood electricity, and there were no refrigerators. Meat spoiled and rotted very quickly in warm weather, so people made spicy, strong-tasting sauces for their food to make the food taste better.

One of the reasons that Columbus sailed to this country from Europe was because the Europeans wanted a quick way to get to the spices in the Far East. Columbus hadn't planned on there being another continent in his way when he sailed west. You might say that America was discovered because of the love people had for spices and herbs!

Herbs, flowers, and the oils from certain plants have been loved for centuries because of their delicious smell. When the baby Jesus was born, three men who were students of the stars and mathematics knew that it was time for a new King to be born. They found the baby and gave him the richest presents that they could. They gave him gold, frankincense, and myrrh. Frankincense and myrrh are the sticky gums that ooze from two different trees in the Middle Eastern countries. The trees are rare, so the gum was hard to find. People put drops of these gums on charcoal fires in little pots and burned them. The burning gum filled the room with a sweet smell. This was a lovely treat for people long ago, and incense is still something we enjoy today.

Catnip

Catnip is a very ancient herb. When you dry the leaves, crush them, and pour boiling water over them, they make catnip tea. If you have a cold and fever, catnip tea can make you sweat a little, cooling your body so the fever goes down. For centuries, catnip tea was used for helping people get over colds and fevers. Catnip tea is supposed to be very good for children too. It produces restful sleep and quiets irritable, restless children when they are sick.

Buy a package of catnip seed from your nursery or a seed catalog. Sow it in good soil or plant it in a large pot, bucket, or flower box. The catnip plant is two feet tall and doesn't need much water.

If you have a cat, be careful. The cat won't bother your catnip unless you pinch the leaves. When the leaves have been pinched or bruised, they give off a pungent odor that a cat loves. Then the cat will tear the catnip plant apart, roll on it, and run around in circles. Cats *love* this herb, so you might plant a pot or two for a cat you know and a pot for you.

When the plant begins to dry and shrivel, pick the leaves and spread them out where no cat can get them. Let them dry. Crumble them into a plastic sack and tie it tightly.

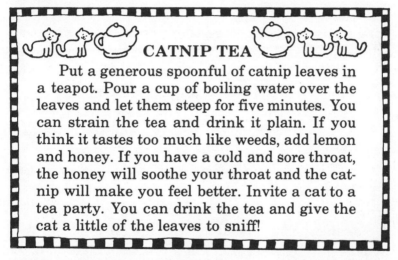

CATNIP TEA

Put a generous spoonful of catnip leaves in a teapot. Pour a cup of boiling water over the leaves and let them steep for five minutes. You can strain the tea and drink it plain. If you think it tastes too much like weeds, add lemon and honey. If you have a cold and sore throat, the honey will soothe your throat and the catnip will make you feel better. Invite a cat to a tea party. You can drink the tea and give the cat a little of the leaves to sniff!

THE SECOND WEEK

PATIENCE

Waiting for your garden to grow is exciting. It does take patience though. Patience is one of the hardest things you must learn to become wise and happy. Patience means waiting for things to happen until it is time for them to happen.

Plants know all about patience. Cherry trees don't throw all the cherries down before they are ripe. The cherry trees flower, grow, their fruit ripens and falls when they are ready to do these things. If the cherry tree didn't do every one of these things, there would be no cherries.

But people forget that we are all part of nature too. We try to make things happen before it is time. We push and shove and try to force things. If you cut open a cocoon to let the butterfly out, the butterfly will die. If you dig up your seeds everyday, they won't be able to grow roots and turn into plants.

FOOD FOR IMPATIENCE

It is hard to wait. Here's how to grow a delicious food that will grow in three or four days, and you can watch it grow.

Take an old, one quart mayonnaise or pickle jar. Buy alfalfa seeds or mung beans at a natural food store or grocery store. Put one tablespoon of seed in the jar. Add three tablespoons of water. Cover the top of the jar with two layers of cheesecloth. Put a rubber band around the top to hold the cheesecloth on. Put the jar on a shelf in a kitchen cupboard where it is dark.

Every day, pour a cup of water in the jar and put the cheesecloth back on. Gently, gently, pour the water out through the cloth.

The seeds should be damp but not sitting in water.

In three or four days, put the jar in the sun for an hour or two. This will make the sprouts green and add vitamins. Sprouts are full of protein and are very healthy to eat.

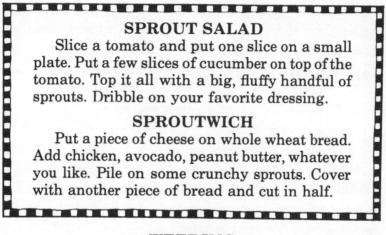

SPROUT SALAD

Slice a tomato and put one slice on a small plate. Put a few slices of cucumber on top of the tomato. Top it all with a big, fluffy handful of sprouts. Dribble on your favorite dressing.

SPROUTWICH

Put a piece of cheese on whole wheat bread. Add chicken, avocado, peanut butter, whatever you like. Pile on some crunchy sprouts. Cover with another piece of bread and cut in half.

WEEDING

I hate to weed. Some people think that gardeners love to spend their days pulling weeds, but I never met one who did.

So. Don't weed. It's too boring. Don't give the weeds space to grow. When you can see a line of seedlings above the ground, take handfuls of grass clippings or hay or straw and make a blanket of them up close to the seedlings. Cover all the bare dirt up, but let the green seedlings stand free so they can get sunlight and air. This is called mulching.

As the seedlings get taller, add more mulch. Put on hay or grass or leaves and gradually build the pile up to be about five or six inches deep. Grass is one of the best mulches because it adds nitrogen to the soil when it dies, which the plants need.

Mulching does a lot of good things. Plants can't grow through a thick mulch, so you don't have to weed. Mulch keeps the soil cooler in summer heat. Mulch keeps the sun from drying up the dirt and evaporating all the water. The soil stays cool and damp under the mulch. You only have to water about half as much when you have a thick mulch all over your garden. Mulch also adds a lot of plant matter to the soil when you turn it under in the fall. This makes better dirt for growing plants next year.

Gardeners who mulch can build a tent over their clothesline with a sheet and sit under it drinking lemonade all day. Gardeners who don't mulch spend all day weeding. I'm a lemonade drinker myself, but maybe you like to weed. It's your garden.

INDOOR MULCHING

Nurseries sell packages of moss that are great for mulching your indoor plants. The moss keeps the pots moist and can be a good thing for your plants, especially if you sometimes forget to water them. The soil will stay damper under the protective mulch.

Indoor gardens also look prettier with a nice mossy covering over the dirt. Go to your plant store and ask. Maybe you could use a little mulch for your indoor garden too.

THE THIRD WEEK

HOW DO THEY DO IT?

Your pea plants are now big enough to have flowers on them. The flowers are very important because it is from the pea flower that the pea pod will grow. Pea pods are the fruits of the pea plant. Peas are the seeds that are in the fruit.

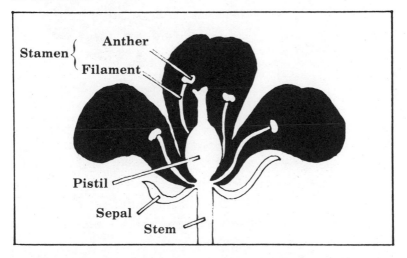

Here is a picture of a flower if we cut it in half from top to bottom. Some flowers are male, some female. Some flowers, like the one above, are both male and female! This means that this one flower can make a fruit without the help of another flower.

The male parts of a flower are called the stamens. Stamens usually have a thin filament that holds up the anther. The anther is powdery yellow because it is covered with pollen. Pollen is the flower's sperm. It is half of what the plant needs to make a fruit.

In the middle of the flower is the female part. It is called the pistil. Here is a drawing of a pistil if you cut it in half:

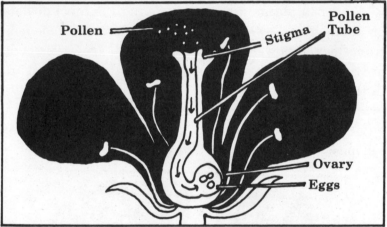

A flower must be fertilized or pollinated for a fruit to grow. When a tiny piece of pollen is blown by the wind or falls into the stigma, it goes down the pollen tube into the ovary where the female egg of the plant is. The pollen and the egg blend together and make a single fruit.

BEES

Are you wondering how a male holly tree ever gets its pollen over to the female flowers on another tree? It is done by insects. Wasps and bees do a wonderful thing for plants. They help pollinate the flowers, spreading the male pollen from flower to flower, so the female pistils will all bear fruit.

Bees are probably the best known pollinators, and you will see many of them crawling in and out of the flowers on your plants. Don't chase them away. The bees are helping the plants grow fruit. Do not shake your hands at the bees or slap at them. They won't sting you if they are not afraid.

Bees are social insects like ants, termites, and wasps. This means that bees live together in groups and raise their children. They aren't like butterflies who lay their eggs on a leaf and fly away. Butterflies are not social animals.

All the eggs in a beehive are laid by the Queen Bee. She is a large female bee whose job it is to lay eggs. The other bees feed her, lick her all over to keep her clean, and take the eggs away so that they can carefully raise the new bees.

You could have twenty different beehives on one farm, and every bee in every hive would always know exactly which hive was its own home, just like you know exactly which house in all the town or which apartment in the city belongs to your family!

How do bees know that? Why don't they get lost and go to the wrong hive?

It all starts with the bees' food. Every bee has a job. The bees you see in your garden are called "worker" bees. All worker bees are young, sexually immature females.

The worker bee flies out every day and gathers nectar, a sweet juice, and pollen from flowers. She sips the nectar up with her long proboscis (sucking organ) and stores it in her crop, a special stomach for nectar.

The pollen sticks to the worker bee's hairy belly as she crawls over the flower. There are stiff spines on the bee's hind legs like combs. With these spines, the bee scrapes the pollen off and stores most of it in a special "basket" that is on the outside of the bee's legs.

The pollen and nectar are taken back to the hive. When one bee meets another bee from the same hive, they both cough up some nectar from their crop and feed each other! It is their way of offering a cup of tea to a friend!

All nectar tastes different to bees, and bees from one hive usually go back to the same gardens every day. Since they are all sharing the same nectar and pollen, the bees from one hive all smell alike! The hive smells like the bees too because the nectar is stored as honey. (The pollen is mixed with a little honey to make stuff called "bee bread," which the bees eat in winter.) A bee would never go in a strange hive because it wouldn't smell right!

The Queen Bee of each hive has her own special smell. The bees lick the Queen to clean her, and they pick up the Queen's smell when they do this job. When bees smell each other, they know that the Queen is alive and healthy because of the scent of their Queen on each other. If the Queen dies, the bees all begin to smell differently to each other. This gives all the bees the message, "The Queen Is Dead." Then they quickly raise a new Queen to lay eggs.

In addition to entertaining us and giving us honey and beeswax, bees pollinate millions of fields every year. Because the bees spread the pollen over the flower, knock it off the anthers into the pistil, carry it from plant to plant, we have squash and tomatoes, figs, apples, cherries and peas. Let's hear it for the bees!

LOOKING

The Arab poet Hafiz, who died in 1390, almost six hundred years ago, wrote:

"The rose is not the rose unless thou see. . . ."

What he meant was that even a rose is not a beautiful, amazing, miraculous thing if you do not *look* at it and *see* it. Some people walk right past things and never see them. Some people don't see flowers and plants. Some people don't see animals or children or even other people. Shut your eyes and think about what you've seen so far today. If you can't think of anything, you may need to look around you more. Look at things and try to really see them.

You can begin with a flower. Find a flower in a garden or a flower shop. Take a pair of scissors and lay the flower on a piece of white paper. Now look at the flower. Turn it around. Smell it. Touch it. Look inside it if you can.

When you have looked at the flower to see what it is like, take the scissors and begin to cut the flower open. Try to find the anthers, the ovary, the small green leaves at the bottom of the ovary that cover the bud when it is closed. See how many parts you can find. It may be a female flower or a male flower. It may have male and female parts. Look at it and try to see it as if it is the first flower you have ever really seen.

THE FOURTH WEEK

WORMS

I didn't like worms much when I was little, but now I really respect earthworms. When I dig in my garden, it makes me smile to see lots of worms being turned up.

I like worms because they do so many jobs for the soil in my garden. Here is a picture of a worm if you were to cut it in half and look at it under a microscope.

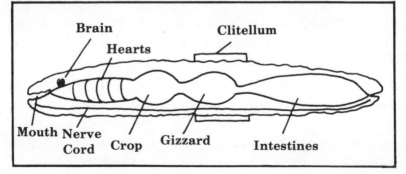

Worms have more parts than you might think. The mouth takes in food. The crop, gizzard, and intestines digest the food. Any unused food comes out the worm's anus. The earthworm has a tiny brain, nerves, and five pairs of hearts! It doesn't need lungs because oxygen from the air can easily go through its thin, damp skin into its blood vessels.

Worms don't see, smell, or hear like we do, but their sense of touch is excellent. They can feel the vibration of you walking above them when they are three feet underground.

Every earthworm can be male or female. Every earthworm can mate with every other earthworm. This is different from dogs and cats and people. Male dogs can only mate and make puppies with female dogs. Female dogs can only mate and make puppies with male dogs, but the earthworm has parts in its body that let it be either male or female!

The earthworm looks smooth, but it is actually covered with stiff bristles, eight on each segment of the worm. These bristles hold onto things so the worm can move. The worm digs in with part of the bristles and drags the rest of its body up to the bristles that are sticking into the ground. A worm can make its body smooth or bristly to help its movements.

Worms do many things for our gardens.

First of all, the worm eats the dirt. It goes in his mouth, and the worm uses some of the minerals and tiny pieces of plants for food. This breaks up the soil into small particles. It makes the soil fluffier, and this is food for plant roots. Roots can grow better in fine soil with no large, hard lumps of dirt.

The worms also eat leaves and decayed plants on the top of the soil. They take the pieces of leaf down deep in the soil and mix it with the hard clay. This makes the garden soil richer.

Worms make tunnels. These tunnels let air and water go down in the soil more easily. Roots need water to grow and the air makes the soil less hard. A garden with lots of earthworms is usually a garden that is good for plants. Some people even buy earthworms in the spring and add them to their gardens to make the soil lighter, more crumbly, and richer.

If your mother ever tells you to go out in the garden and eat worms when she is mad at you, don't do it! Worms are too good for the gardens to waste them by eating them. Go out instead and love your worms.

If you want to see how worms help plants, you can try this. Take two large flower pots and put some dirt from your garden in each pot. Plant a small marigold seedling in each pot.

Dig up a couple of worms up from your garden. Put them on top of the soil of one pot. Sprinkle the pots with water and make sure the worms have dug into one pot. Put both pots where they will get the same amount of sun, and put a dish under the pot with the worms in it. Then they won't crawl out the hole in the bottom. Water them regularly. Worms need water. The pot with the worms should grow a larger, stronger marigold. (If it doesn't, maybe the worms have escaped.) Watch the pots for a month and see if the worms make a difference.

JULY

Summer has come,
  healthy and free,
Whence the brown
  wood is bent to
  the ground:
The slender nimble
  deer leap,
And the path of
  seals is smooth.

—Anonymous

JULY

THE FIRST WEEK

The Immortal Toad—A Chinese Legend

Once there was a great archer named Yi. He had been given a magic bow when the world was being burned up by ten suns in the heavens. Yi had used the bow to shoot nine of the suns out of the sky and had saved the world.

Since he was such a great archer, the emperor sent Yi to kill a demon who had caused a river to flood the country. Yi shot the evil demon, but he spared a beautiful woman who was with the demon. This woman was Heng-o, and she became Yi's wife.

Now Heng-o was very vain. She was frightened of becoming old and losing her good looks. One day Heng-o crept into Yi's private box of magical things and stole his magic potion that enabled the drinker to live forever.

When Yi discovered that his wife had stolen the potion and had drunk all of it, he was very angry. Heng-o fled, running all the way to the moon where she was turned into a toad for her silly vanity. Chinese children used to believe that there is an immortal toad—Heng-o—living in the moon.

TOADS, GOOD OR BAD?

Did you ever hear that toads can cause warts if you touch them? People all over the world have been suspicious of toads because the toad is not very beautiful to look at unless you happen to be a mother toad. Some people believed that toads are evil. They believed that witches and the devil loved toads, but good people hated them.

Toads are really wonderful creatures. I like them, and if that makes me a witch, it's all right with me.

Toads become very frightened if you pick them up. When you are frightened, you might scream. Toads can't scream or bite or claw, but they can secrete a whitish liquid from their skin. This liquid comes from two glands behind the toad's eyes. It won't make you warty, like the toad, but the liquid can sting a little. This liquid is the toad's only protection. Dogs and cats usually leave toads alone, because the liquid burns their mouths.

Toads are one of the gardener's best friends. Nearly all of the food a toad eats is insects, and nearly all these insects can hurt your plants. In the three months of summer, a toad will eat 10,000 insects! Toads in your garden are a lot better than spraying your garden with poisons to kill the insects.

July / 107

Toads begin their life in a pond or stream. The eggs are laid in a jellylike spiral. The female toad lays thousands of eggs at one time. Sometimes the narrow string of eggs is seventy feet long.

In a few days, tadpoles hatch from the eggs. At this time, the amazing thing is that tadpoles look like fatheaded tiny fish. But in six to nine weeks the tadpoles have grown hind legs, then front legs, and their mouths have gotten bigger. Their long tails shrink up into their body. They are tiny toads, not even a half-inch long.

Then the toads hop onto dry land and hide for a week or two. The first time it rains, the toads pop out from every rock and bush and scatter over the land. People used to say it was "raining toads" because of the way toads suddenly appeared in a spring rainstorm.

If there is a toad living near your garden, don't scare him away. Be gentle with your toad, and maybe he'll stick around.

PEAS AND CARROTS

You should be harvesting your peas about now. Peas are just great to eat raw, fresh off the bush. They are tender and sweet.

Peas are good steamed in a steamer or cooked in just a little water for five minutes till they are barely tender.

It's almost a shame to put anything on fresh peas except a dab of butter.

Try cooking sliced carrots for about twenty minutes in water. Cook your peas for five minutes when the carrots are done. Strain the water off of the vegetables. Mix them up together with butter. The orange and green colors of the carrots and peas are very beautiful together. Try to serve your vegetables so they look beautiful as well as being good to eat. It is nice to feed your eyes when you feed your stomach.

THE SECOND WEEK

Silly Jack—An Old Irish Tale

Once upon a time there was a man named Jack who lived in Ireland. Now Jack was a great trickster and also a drunkard. He drank every night and then amused himself by making fun of the Devil.

Jack grew old, and the Devil waited to claim his soul, but Jack tricked the Devil. One night,

Jack cleverly made the Devil promise that he would not claim Jack's soul for ten years. The Devil promised, but Jack died the next day.

Since the Devil couldn't take his soul, Jack went to Heaven's Gate, but the huge, golden gate would not open for Jack's wicked soul.

Jack couldn't get into Hell. He couldn't get into Heaven. He was lost in the darkness until the Devil took pity on him and threw him a live coal from Hell. Jack put the lit coal in a hollowed-out turnip that he had been eating, and it gave a light for him to see by.

Jack wanders the earth even now, carrying his poor lantern, and sometimes you can see him at Halloween time, a lost soul with no place to go.

JACK-O'-LANTERNS

There weren't any pumpkins growing in Ireland when Jack lived, so the people hollowed out turnips and put small candles in them for lanterns. When the settlers got to North America, they discovered a new fruit that was delicious to eat and perfect for jack-o'-lanterns. It was the pumpkin.

Pumpkins are part of the squash family. They grow long, trailing vines and bear huge, orange fruit that we eat in pie, stewed or baked. If you want to grow a Halloween pumpkin, it is time to start.

Planting Pumpkins

There are several different kinds of pumpkin seed. Most kinds of pumpkin grow on a large vine that takes up a lot of room, but there is one kind that is perfect for small gardens or apartment gardens. It is called a Cinderella pumpkin. It grows into a bushy plant with two pumpkins about ten inches in diameter. If you live in an apartment with a sunny window, you can try growing a Cinderella pumpkin plant.

If you are growing plants outdoors, you will need a spot three feet by four feet for a pumpkin hill, or you can plant a bush or two of Cinderella pumpkins in a smaller space.

Prepare the ground for either kind of pumpkin the same way. Make a hill with the dirt. Add manure or compost (if you have any) to the hill. Pat the top of the hill a little flat and plant four or five pumpkin seeds in a circle, about three inches apart, one inch deep. Cover the seed and water the hill occasionally.

In about eight to ten days, two leaves will poke up. They are the first leaves, or seed leaves, because they came right out of the seed. From them sprouts a different looking leaf. The two seed leaves feed the plant until other leaves can grow. Then the plant doesn't need the seed leaves, and they dry up and fall off.

The pumpkin plant has two different kinds of flowers, male and female. The male flowers are on a long stem. The female flowers sit on a short stem with a round, green knob right under the flower. The green knob is the female flower's ovary. It will grow into a pumpkin when the bees carry pollen from the male flower's stamen into the female pistil.

If you are growing your pumpkin indoors, you will have to become a bee if you want any pumpkins! Get a small paintbrush like one in a watercolor set. When the male flower is grown, look inside it. Do you see the anther covered with a fuzz of yellow pollen? Touch the paintbrush to the pollen until you have some grains of pollen on the tip. Then wipe the pollen off inside the female flower. Shake the brush lightly so some pollen falls down on the sticky stigma in the middle of the female flower. Do this every day for a few days. When your teacher asks you in September what you did this summer, you can say that you became a bee!

If your pumpkins are outside, put hay or grass clippings five or six inches deep all around the young pumpkin plants. When the pumpkins are large enough to sit on the hay, put a piece of cardboard under them to discourage bugs. If you want one really big pumpkin, wait until the pumpkins are small, green knobs. Then cut every green pumpkin off the plant except for one. *Just cut the pumpkin's stem.* Don't cut the main vine. The pumpkin you leave will get all the food from the plant and grow very large.

DRINKING SALAD (GAZPACHO)

When your tomatoes and cucumbers are ready, try this "salad" that you can drink.

Put into a blender:

1 cucumber, peeled and chopped
One half of a medium onion, chopped
2 large tomatoes, peeled and chopped
One half of a clove of garlic
One and one-half cups of cold water (or tomato juice)
One and one-half tablespoons of red wine vinegar
One teaspoon salt
One tablespoon of olive oil
One half-cup finely crushed bread crumbs (French bread makes great crumbs)

Put the top tightly on the blender. Turn on and blend until everything is fairly smooth. Chill in the refrigerator until very cold. Serve in small bowls with a little chopped cucumber on top.

The Beautiful Maiden—
An American Indian Story

nce upon a time there was the most beautiful young woman in the world living among the people who plant corn. She was so beautiful and she loved herself so much that she would not marry any of the young men in her tribe.

But one day, a handsome stranger appeared. She fell in love with him and followed him away from her people to be his wife. They walked a long, long way to his bark wigwam and lived happily for a while.

One day the young man returned from hunting deer, and he was very tired. His magic powers were weak because of the long hunt. As his beautiful wife smoothed his hair, he turned into his true shape—a huge snake.

The poor young woman ran from the wigwam, but the snake followed. She ran and ran, but she could not escape.

Seeing her terror, the Thunder god took pity on her. The young woman saw before her three shining men. The tallest threw a glittering spear at the snake and killed it. The young woman was amazed. A black cloud grew around the men and the young woman.

The spearthrower was Thunder himself, and the two other men were his sons. The beautiful maiden married the youngest son, and they had a baby boy. This baby also had the power to throw lightning and make thunder.

One day, the young woman wanted to visit her mother on earth and show her young son to her tribe. Thunder warned the young woman that she could go, but the boy must never shoot his arrows on earth. The boy's arrows were lightning and could burn up the tribe.

The visit was a great success and all the tribe was glad to see the young woman and her handsome young son. Everything was going well, but one day the boy became upset. The other boys in the village had teased him because he never shot his arrows and hunted rabbits and birds with the children of the village.

Angry, the son of Thunder shot an arrow into the forest. The crash of the arrow nearly knocked down the other boys, and part of the forest caught on fire.

His father, the Thunder god, came down to earth in a huge, dark cloud and carried the Thunder Boy away so he could not hurt the people.

WATER

I never paid much attention to thunder and lightning until I moved from the center of the United States to the West Coast. There is almost never any thunder and lightning around San Francisco, and I miss it terribly. It is exciting when it has been very hot and dry, and the air begins to get heavier, almost yellow. Then you can hear thunder, a gentle boom far away. The air gets darker, clouds cover the sky, and the thunder seems to be right over your head. The rain pours down, and lightning looks like it is breaking open the sky.

If it rains a lot where you live, you won't have to water your plants much. If you live in an apartment, you have to be the rain god for your plants and water them whenever their leaves droop or the dirt around them is dry.

Many people live in dry parts of our country where there is little rain in the summer. They have had to invent clever ways of conserving water.

The Zuni Indians of western New Mexico plant their squash and corn and vegetables in fields that look like waffles. The people shape the dirt into neat, square areas about a foot across with walls of dirt around the square. All the squares together look like a huge dirt waffle. These "waffles" let the rain water run down into the squares. It is a very smart idea for a dry climate.

Watering Your Plants

From the first planting of a seed until the plant is fully grown and the fruiting and flowering is over, every plant needs water. Water in the soil dissolves minerals, and then the plant can absorb them through tiny hairs on the roots. These minerals pass through the root hairs up the root to feed the stems and leaves of the plant. Roots reach down and outward into the soil because they are looking for water.

Read your seed packages carefully. They will tell you about watering your plants. If the package doesn't tell you, ask at a nursery. By watering your garden carefully, you will have strong, healthy plants that produce more vegetables and flowers.

THE FOURTH WEEK

A Good Bug

Once there was a bug that was very good. It never bit when children held it but crawled gently over their fingers. It was brightly colored and beautiful like a new toy, and the bug ate only the insects that hurt gardeners' plants. Everyone loved this bug so much that they gave it a special name. They called the bug the "ladybug" in honor of a great lady, the Virgin Mary, mother of the baby Jesus. It was a great honor to be named for the Virgin Mary, but the

ladybug has always lived up to its name. It is gentle and good and helps us live.

LADYBUGS

Many years ago, after the harvest, the farmers would burn the old vines and plants to clear the fields for next year. The children would chant:

> Ladybug, Ladybug, fly away home!
> Your house is on fire,
> Your children will burn!

Very young ladybugs cannot fly, so the children were right.

Ladybugs are very neatly made insects. They have six legs, a body, a shield that is at the end of the body, and a head partly hidden by the shield. The body is usually red with black spots on it.

The ladybug's body is very interesting. When a ladybug crawls around on your finger, you would never know that it has wings. The wings are neatly folded up under the red back, which is really a two-part wing cover. The hard wing cover protects the delicate wings until the ladybug is frightened or startled. Then the lady bug holds up the covers and unfolds her wings. The wing covers stay up and still, and the wings move so fast, there is only a blur while the ladybug flies. When she lands, she looks very messy with her wings sticking out of the wing covers. She folds them up quickly, tucks them in, and is once more a neat red and black ladybug.

Ladybugs once saved all the orange trees in California! An insect called the mealy bug was destroying the orange trees. There are also orange trees in Australia, but no mealy bugs because of the Australian ladybug. Hundreds of ladybugs were sent from Australia to California. They ate the mealy bugs and saved all of California's orange trees in two years' time.

Don't ever kill ladybugs. They are friends to every gardener. They eat aphids and other bugs that damage your plants and flowers. When there are ladybugs in your garden, most of the pests will disappear.

The Great Ladybug Hunt

Have a ladybug hunt. Invite your friends. Make a pitcher of lemonade to drink after the hunt and tell every friend to bring a clean jar with a tight top. Tell them to punch holes in the top so the ladybugs can breathe. Offer prizes for the most ladybugs captured. Let your friends hunt all over the neighborhood for an hour. Tell them to be careful with the ladybugs and not to crush them. At the end of the hunt, take each jar and dump the ladybugs out gently near the stems of the plants in your garden.

Be gentle so the ladybugs won't fly away. They will

eat the pests on your vegetables and flowers. Don't forget to let them out of the jars right away. Bugs don't like being in jars any more than you would.

THE PRAYING MANTIS

Now this is a weird insect, really weird. It is a good insect to have in the garden because it eats up plant-destroying bugs and caterpillars. It is a very hungry creature. Some people think it should be called the "prey-ing" mantis because it preys on other bugs. It does look like it is praying, though, when it sits quietly on a branch with its "hands" folded together.

The mantis is born from a brown egg case. The female mantis wraps the case around a twig as she is making it. The egg case looks just like a lump on the twig, which protects it from birds. Anywhere from fifty to four hundred baby mantis come out of a single egg case.

They are tiny and you can almost see through their cellophanelike bodies. They have a tiny cord like a lifeline tied to them that protects them from falling to the ground. When they are strong enough, the line breaks, and off they go. They begin to eat immediately. They will even fight and eat each other if they can! They eat everything but ants, and the ants, oddly enough, like to eat baby mantis and are their worst enemy!

The mantis has no bones in its body. When it grows larger, it sheds its hard outer coat and the soft inner layer soon hardens and becomes the new hard outer coat.

The mantis has a compound eye. That means that there are many eyes in one large eye. It can see in nearly every direction at once, up, down, almost completely behind itself too! The big, bulging eyes on the side of the mantis' head are the same color as its body during the day. At night, these eyes turn black. There are three more eyes, little ones above the antennas, called ocelli. These eyes cannot see but tell the mantis whether it is night or day, light or dark.

The Mantis in Your Garden

If you want a praying mantis in your garden, you can order the egg cases from one of the large seed companies or get them at an organic gardening center. The cases will be mailed to you in the early spring, and you can tie them tightly to a twig on a bush in your yard. If there are any ants around, put a couple of circles of tape, *sticky side out,* around the limb further down. The ants don't like to go over the sticky tape.

In the spring, the baby mantis will come out. Maybe one will live in your garden. If it does, try feeding it. Pinch off a piece of raw hamburger meat (mantis do not like cooked food) with tweezers and offer it to your mantis. See if he will eat it.

AUGUST

Green, Green, I
want you green
Green the wind
and green the
boughs,
The ship upon the
ocean seen.

—Federico Garcia
Lorca

AUGUST

THE FIRST WEEK

THE PEACEFUL TRIBE

The Wampanong Indians lived near the ocean in the forests of Massachusetts and Rhode Island. They were a peaceful, joyous people who lived in dome-shaped wigwams made of bent young trees and birch bark. They hunted and fished, sang songs, and loved games. It was these people who helped the Pilgrims learn to plant their fields in the 1620s because the Wampanong Indians knew how to grow crops in the new land the Pilgrims had come to.

There was one Indian, a young man named Squanto, who was very friendly to the white men. He helped them trade goods with the Indian tribes and was a good friend. The white men were not good friends to Squanto though. They kidnapped Squanto and took him to Spain. He was going to be sold as a slave when some Spanish monks found him. They helped Squanto get on a ship to England, hoping that he could then sail from England back to Massachusetts.

It took a long time, but Squanto finally managed to return to this country. It was a sad return. While Squanto was gone, the people of his village had all died from a great sickness.

Now, you would think that after all this, Squanto would hate all white men and women, but Squanto was an unusual person. He joined up with Massasoit who was then chief of the Wampanong Indians, and he did not hate anyone.

Squanto was one of the Indians who felt sorry for the Pilgrims. They were trying to plant the same way they had planted back in England. The Pilgrims weren't used to the corn and squashes of Massachusetts, and they didn't know how to plant in the stony soil of the New Land. Squanto knew that the Pilgrims would die if they didn't plant the corn correctly and dry it for the coming winter.

He showed them how to make a mound of earth and bury several small fish in the mound. Then the corn seeds were planted in the top of the mound. The fish were a rich fertilizer that the corn plants used as they grew. It was a new way of planting for the Pilgrims, and they had good harvests because of Squanto's help.

Squanto was a great man. He could love people even when he had been hurt by them. He was one of the truly great Americans.

THE OCEAN AND THE LAND

Nothing in your body works by itself. As you sit reading this, your lungs are going in and out, your heart is pumping blood, your stomach is digesting the last thing that you ate. All the parts of your body work together. If you took out any important part, it would be hard for you to stay healthy.

The whole world is like that. The seas and the land work together to grow plants. Because of the great oceans, large amounts of water evaporate upward. Much of this water forms clouds that blow over the land and give rain to the plants. Without the oceans, all the land would soon be dry and barren. We would have no rain, so plants wouldn't grow. We would be hungry and so would all the other animals and insects.

The ocean needs the land too. On coastal areas, in tide pools, grows some of the ocean life that feeds other creatures that live in the sea. Without the tide pools, larger fish wouldn't have any food. Underground springs flow up and become streams. The streams flow into rivers that dump their water into the oceans. So the water that floods over the land when it rains goes back to the ocean where it came from originally. It is like a circle.

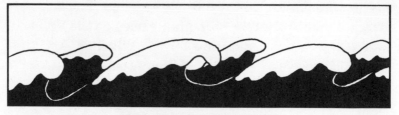

HUNGRY BURROS

Julius Caesar was a leader of the Roman people who lived in Italy about 2025 years ago. He decided to make war on a country in North Africa, so all the soldiers and their equipment were loaded into ships. Burros were put on the ships to carry the gear when the soldiers landed.

When the ships got to North Africa, there was no grain and hay left for the burros. The Roman soldiers waded out into the ocean and harvested seaweed. They carried it up onto the shore and washed all the salt water off with clear, clean water. The burros ate the seaweed and survived. The ocean fed them!

PLANTS AND SEAWEED

If you live near an ocean there is great fertilizer you can get free. Gather seaweed off the beach. Rinse it off with a hose and chop it up. Use it as mulch on your plants or add it to your compost pile.

Seaweed contains the minerals that you find in the sea. About sixteen percent of most seaweed is made up of minerals like potassium, sulphates, and calcium. As the plants rot in the dirt, these minerals are added to your garden. They are great for the soil.

If you don't live near the ocean, you can buy ground-up kelp (seaweed) and fertilizers made from fish at your nursery. Be careful when you are using fish fertilizer in the house. I once used fish fertilizer on my house plants, and it really did smell FISHY. It was all right though. I just pretended for a few days that I was Jonah and my smelly house was the belly of the great fish that swallowed him. It made me a lot more sympathetic toward Jonah.

THE SECOND WEEK

The Giant Turnip—A Russian Tale

 nce upon a time there was a grandmother and grandfather living in a little house with a little garden around it in a little village. Grandfather went out in the garden one day and planted the small seed of a turnip.

"Grandmother," he said, "I have planted the small seed of a turnip in the garden. It is such a very small seed that we may be able to grow a very small turnip to put in the soup pot this winter."

Grandmother was very glad, because the winters were long and cold, and a good pot of soup was always delicious when the snow stood six feet deep outside.

"Good for you, Grandfather," she said, and every day Grandmother watered the turnip seed.

The seed sprouted leaves, and they grew thick and green until the winter was coming down upon the village with its cold breath.

Grandmother felt the chill in her bones and wanted to make a pot of good soup. "The turnip is just the thing for my soup," she said. So she went out in the garden to pull it.

But no matter how hard Grandmother pulled, the turnip wouldn't budge from the ground.

"Grandfather," she called. "Come help me pull up our turnip."

So Grandfather came and grabbed Grandmother by the waist and they both pulled, but the turnip wouldn't budge.

Grandfather went next door and asked his great friend Piotr to come help, and Piotr grabbed Grandfather's waist and pulled.

Grandfather grabbed Grandmother, and Grandmother held onto the green turnip top, but the turnip wouldn't budge.

Finally two tiny mice, a brown one and a gray one, crawled out of the haystack in the corner of the garden. "If you will give us some good soup this winter when the snow is six feet deep," said the gray one (who wasn't very shy), "we will help you pull the turnip out."

Grandfather and Grandmother didn't see how two tiny mice could be much help, and they laughed.

"All right," Grandmother said. "I will give you soup all winter if you can help us pull the turnip."

Grandmother grabbed the green turnip top. Grandfather grabbed Grandmother. Piotr held onto Grandfather. The gray mouse held onto Piotr's pants cuff and the brown mouse (who was shy) held onto the gray mouse's tail, and they all pulled.

Suddenly, with a great POP, the turnip flew into the air. Everyone fell down on the ground in a pile, and the brown mouse was so frightened it ran back into the hay.

The turnip was so big that it made enough soup for Grandmother, Grandfather, their neighbor Piotr, the gray mouse and the brown mouse all winter long, and everyone was warm and full while the snow piled up six feet deep and the winter wind howled.

TURNIPS

When you pull up and harvest your onions and garlic, turnips are a good crop to plant around the edge of your garden.

Dig some compost or manure into the ground and plant the turnip seed about one quarter of an inch deep. Do not bury it too deeply or it won't come up. Water the seeds gently. Thin the plants by pulling some out when they grow up so that there is three inches between the green tops. This gives the turnip space to grow underground. Turnips like water, so mulch them when you have thinned them and keep the soil moist.

THE THIRD WEEK

HOW PLANTS EAT

Now that you have been eating from your garden for weeks, have you ever wondered how a plant eats? You know that plants stop growing when they are in a dark closet with no light or sun. Plants also stop growing if it is very cold and when they get no water. If you could put a plant in a vacuum chamber (a tightly sealed jar with no holes or leaks except for the pump) and pumped all the air out, you would discover that the plant soon dies when there is no air around it. Plants need air, water, sun, and soil, but how do they make their food?

If you could look at a leaf under a microscope, it would look like this.

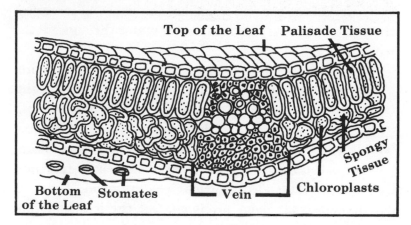

A leaf is a miracle that happens all around us. It is made up of several parts. On the top of a leaf is a protective cover. Then there are hundreds and thousands of tightly packed cells. These cells are called "palisade" tissue. Palisades were huge fences made by lining up logs on end around a village. The palisade cells are tightly lined up like walls in the leaf. Inside the palisade cells are tiny things called chloroplasts. Chloroplasts have a substance called chlorophyll in them. This makes chloroplasts all green.

Under the palisade cells is a spongy section. It, too, contains chloroplasts and is full of spaces for air. On the underneath surface of the leaf are holes like mouths called stomates. The whole leaf is crisscrossed with tiny veins. You can see the larger veins without a microscope.

All of these parts of a leaf do different jobs so the plant can live. The top of the leaf protects the cells inside. The stomates, the mouths, breathe in the air. Air is made up of oxygen and carbon dioxide, two gases. The spongy tissue holds the air and takes out the carbon dioxide for the plant to use it. The veins send water throughout the leaf.

The palisade and spongy tissues hold the chloroplasts, and it is the tiny chloroplasts that do an amazing thing. The chloroplasts are like miniature ovens floating in the cells of a leaf. When the sun hits the surface of the leaf, it is like turning on the ovens in a leaf. The chloroplasts use the sun's light and heat to make energy. When the sun shines on a leaf, the leaf's ovens go on. It doesn't get hot like your oven at home, but the leaf now has enough energy to make food.

To make its food, the plant must take water from the soil and carry it up to the leaf. The leaf breathes in air through its stomates and uses the carbon dioxide. The leaf takes the water and carbon dioxide, uses the sun for energy, and makes a sugar that is its food. This process is called photosynthesis.

The plant not only makes sugar for its food, it also breathes out oxygen at the end of this process. Animals need oxygen to breathe, so we are all grateful to plants for making the air around us full of oxygen. If you drew a picture of what happens when a leaf makes food, it would look like this.

CARBON DIOXIDE + WATER +
    SUNLIGHT (ENERGY) = SUGAR AND OXYGEN

WATER

Plants need water. Break a leaf off of a plant in your garden. In a few hours, it will be very limp. It is limp because there is no water going into the leaf. When a leaf draws in water, it is like filling a balloon with water. The balloon is limp, but as water fills it up, it gets tight and hard. When a leaf gets enough water, the water fills all the cells in the leaf with moisture and makes the leaf stiff. If you put the leaf in water, it might suck up enough liquid to be firm again.

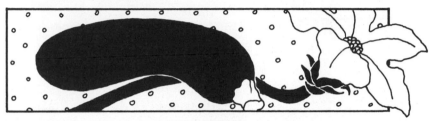

ZUCCHINI

When your zucchini ripen, try this for a pre-dinner snack.

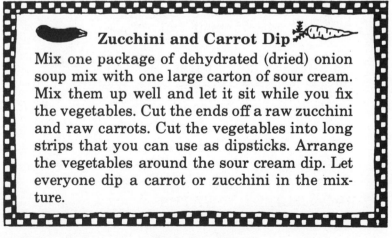

Zucchini and Carrot Dip
Mix one package of dehydrated (dried) onion soup mix with one large carton of sour cream. Mix them up well and let it sit while you fix the vegetables. Cut the ends off a raw zucchini and raw carrots. Cut the vegetables into long strips that you can use as dipsticks. Arrange the vegetables around the sour cream dip. Let everyone dip a carrot or zucchini in the mixture.

The Green Cup Legend

nce upon a time there was an angel named Satan who grew tired of Heaven. He was tired of serving God, so he gathered some other angels together and they made war against God. The good angel, Michael, led God's forces and defeated Satan. During the battle, Michael struck a great blow to Satan's head and knocked his crown off. A beautiful green stone fell to earth from this crown.

This green stone was more beautiful than any stone that had ever been found on earth, and a great artist who found it hollowed it out and made a cup from it. Legend says that when Jesus had his last supper before he was killed, he drank out of this green cup.

A very old word for bowl was "grail," and the cup was called The Holy Grail from then on. People believed that if you could find the Holy Grail, God would love you very much, so Christian people searched everywhere for this green cup. It was hard to find the Holy Grail. Only a person who was pure in their thoughts, their words, and their deeds could ever see the Holy Grail.

People believed that the brilliant, glowing

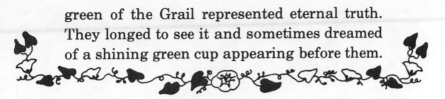

green of the Grail represented eternal truth.
They longed to see it and sometimes dreamed
of a shining green cup appearing before them.

GREEN

Green is a very special color. The Ancient Egyptians used green-colored cloth to wrap up sick people. The green color was supposed to cure certain sicknesses. Green is so nice to look at, so soothing to the eyes, that the ancient Persians tried to cure eye diseases by having their patients look at green jewels and colors.

In the Koran, the sacred book of Mohammedans, it is promised that after death the good people will be rewarded with richly blooming gardens of a dark green color. The ancient Greeks chose green to stand for Aphrodite, the Goddess of Love, and the Romans did the same, choosing green for Venus, Goddess of Love and the Springtime.

Because everything is brown and gray in winter, green is the color of hope for it promises new buds and leaves, new food and beauty for people. Green is the color of new beginnings and joy, of the wonder, miracle and pain of growth. Green is the color of children everywhere.

CLUBS

Clubs are fun. A club can be any group of people who want to meet together and do things. Maybe you would like to have a gardening club. If you have any friends who like to grow things, you could meet once a month and have fun. Here are some of the things you could do.

1. Go on a garden tour. Visit each others' gardens and see what you are all doing.
2. Visit a garden or park in your town. Call the park department and see if someone will talk to your club about how the gardeners take care of the park.
3. Cook and eat some of the food you have grown. Have a pot-luck supper and let everyone bring something they have grown.
4. Walk around your neighborhood. Start a leaf collection with all the club members contributing or a bird book with a list of birds that you have seen.
5. Have pumpkin and zucchini contests. See who can grow the biggest one.
6. Forage for compost together. Take plastic sacks and gather leaves and grass clippings. Share them.
7. Have a work day and help each other with your plants.
8. Have a good time, giggle, talk, run around, and enjoy the summer.

SEPTEMBER

The Vegetative
Universe opens
like a flower
from the earth's
center
in which is
eternity . . .
—William Blake

SEPTEMBER

THE FIRST WEEK

AUTUMN

Now it is September. If you live in the southern half of the country, it is still hot. Your plants are growing well. You can plant another row of radishes if you want. The nights are getting longer and colder. In the northern states, trees are changing, the leaves are turning yellow, the air is getting cooler.

It is nice to think back during the winter and remember your garden. Maybe next year you can get a camera and take pictures of your garden while it grows and changes. You can sit in front of your plants and ask someone to take a picture of you and your garden too. You grow and change like your plants do, not as fast as a zucchini or a radish, but slowly, just the way you should.

Growing is living. It takes time and patience. Sometimes it is fun. Sometimes it is boring. Sometimes it feels good, sometimes it hurts, but whether you feel good or feel bad, you know that you are alive. Being alive means being bored, having fun, waiting patiently, harvesting at the end, succeeding and having failures. Being alive is changing every day, moving and being still. In a way it doesn't matter whether the day is happy or not. What counts is how you use this day to move on to the next one, how you use this moment to become something else during the next moment.

Being alive is not only feeling. It is caring for things, helping them, protecting them, using them, enjoying them. This is love. When you water your garden, collect grass and leaves for mulch, tie up the tomato plants, harvest the fruit and eat it, enjoy watching it grow, you are loving.

Love is a habit, just like eating eggs for breakfast every single morning or biting your fingernails. Habits come about because you do them a lot. When you do something all the time, whether it is knitting, playing football, or reading, you get better and better at it. It can become a habit. When you love things, you get better and better at loving.

Gardeners are lovers. They make beautiful things where none were before. They grow food to feed their friends and family. A garden is a work of love.

A STRANGE PLANT

Do you know what a poem is? A poem is like a tomato. In order to get a tomato, you have to prepare the ground, buy seed, make compost, water the plants, tie them up, and harvest them. When you put together all of these things, you get a round, red tomato. A poem is like everything you know coming together to say something in just a few lines so that it sounds special. You put together all that you have seen and heard and tasted and touched and felt about things around you and get a small group of words that tell this to other people. Giving someone a poem is like giving them a tomato.

Think back on your garden and all you have done with it. See if you can remember a special moment or something that was very beautiful or funny or surprising.

It might be fun for you to write down and describe a plant or a special thing that happened while you gardened. It could be a long poem, a very short poem, or several different poems.

Think back to the best plant you raised. Try to make us see it, smell it, almost taste it with your words. If you can, it will be as if a special poem grew out of your summer garden. Write out your poem. When you read it years from now, you will remember the summer.

Perhaps you will have children when you are grown. You can't save vegetables for your children, but you can write a poem. The poem will be a special thing for later, a memory of who you were during this last summer.

THE SECOND WEEK

CIRCLES

There is nothing in the world that can stand completely alone. Earthworms need the soil. Birds need earthworms for food. People need birds to eat billions of insects so that our food will grow, so people need earthworms too! We don't eat worms, or dirt, but we need worms to feed birds which protect our crops. It is like a circle.

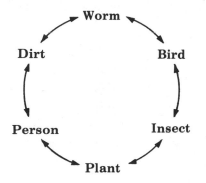

The circle can get bigger if you think about it. The worms, birds, plants, and people need air, clean water, sunlight, darkness, other plants, and animals. The circle grows and grows. People need rain for their crops, so you could put something as large as the ocean into the circle. We need bacteria, which are so tiny you can't see them, to rot the leaves and make new soil. There are things that could go in the circle that we couldn't even see because of their size.

Some people think that human beings aren't in the circle. They see people standing outside like angry children who won't play a game. This is silly. Even if people pretend that they are outside the circle, whatever they do affects everything else that is in the circle.

When farmers used a poison called DDT on their plants to kill bugs, they didn't know what it would do to the circle of all living things. After DDT had been used for years, some birds began to die. The birds had eaten the bugs sprayed with poison. The poision became part of the birds' bodies. When these birds laid their eggs, the poison made the eggshells thin and brittle. Before the baby birds could hatch, the eggs cracked and spoiled. Many birds died.

When factories made things and dumped all their old chemicals and trash in the ocean, no one cared. Factories weren't in the circle, people said. But then rivers became stinking and polluted. The fish died, and those that lived had swallowed enough chemicals to make people sick if they ate them.

Life is a circle. It is alive. It chirps and squeaks and barks and sighs and talks and sometimes stands as silently as oak trees on a winter night. When you don't care about the world, you break the circle, and you can't break a circle without stopping the flow of living things.

It is hard to build bridges over the broken pieces, so be an alive person. Join the circle!

CONNECTIONS

Write down what your plants needed to live during the summer. (Don't forget that they needed *you*!)

Write down what *you* needed to stay alive and well all summer.

THE THIRD WEEK

CHECKLISTS

Now the gardening season is almost over. This is a good time to think about what happened in your garden.

Here is a list of questions. If you write out the answers, you will have a guide for planting and growing for next year.

- Did you have trouble digging up your garden?
- Was the soil hard?
- Did you plant some seed, and then it didn't come up? What kind of seed?
- What plants did really well in your garden?
- What was your most beautiful plant?
- What vegetables were your favorites to eat?
- Did you have lots of weeds?
- Did mulching help fight off the weeds?
- How often did you have to water your garden to keep the plants healthy?
- What plants needed the most water? The least water?

- Do you want to plant more flowers next year? What kind?
- Do you want a larger garden next summer?
- If you grew plants indoors, what were some of your problems?
- Did you like gardening? Do you want to do it again next year?

THE FOURTH WEEK

BOOKS AND CATALOGUES

Winter is one of the nicest times for gardeners. When it is too cold out to grow plants, you can go to school, play with your friends, and be an "armchair" gardener. Armchair gardeners just sit in a chair and think about what they will do next year. It is really fun. You will be surprised how many books there are in the library about gardens, plants, and growing things.

If you want to find a book about something you are interested in, ask someone older or a librarian to help you. Better yet, just poke around and see what you can find. Libraries are like treasure hunts. You never know what you'll find just by looking at the shelves.

Looking up things in a library is a never-ending game. You start with Ladybugs, and when you find a book, there may be a book near it on the shelf with a great picture of a spider on the cover. So you take both of them. Then you get interested in insects and you see another book about worms on the shelf below. This sort of learning experience goes on all throughout the winter, and throughout your whole life.

FREE GOODIES

Here is a list of catalogues that you can send for. Most of them are free. Just write a letter asking for the catalogue by name and send the letter off. You will get a lot of nice things to look through and some ideas for what you can do with your garden. Catalogues are great to look at because of all the strange, new things you learn about when you read them. Maybe you will decide to grow a garden next year that has in it only those flowers and vegetables that you've never seen before!

W. Atlee Burpee Co.
300 Park Avenue
Warminster, Pa. 18974

Stokes Seeds Inc.
Box 548
Buffalo, N.Y. 14240
(This catalog is good for gardeners in northern colder states.)

Thompson & Morgan
Box 100
Farmingdale, N.J. 07727
(This catalog gives you the nutritional information about every vegetable.)

Joseph Harris Company
Moreton Farm
Rochester, N.Y. 14624

Geo. W. Park Seed Co.
Greenwood
South Carolina 29647

Otis S. Twilley
Salisbury, Maryland 21801
(This is a very good catalog for Southern gardeners.)

Stark Bros.
Louisiana, MO 63353
(This is mainly fruits.)

Gurney Seed &
Nursery Co.
Yankton
South Dakota 57078
(This company will supply you with blue potatoes, black corn, yellow radishes, golden beets, round carrots, if you want to grow them!)

Raynor's Berry Book
Salisbury
Maryland 21801
(This is berries and fruits
and nuts.)

R. H. Shumway
628 Cedar Street
Rockford, Ill. 61101
(This catalog uses an-
tique line etchings of the
vegetables and looks just
like an old-fashioned seed
catalog that was printed
before the invention of
photography.)

Seedway, Inc.
Hall, N.Y. 14463
(This is good for garden-
ers in the Northeast of the
country.)

Jackson & Perkins
Medford, Oregon 97501
(They have a spectacular
rose catalog as well as
seeds. Get on their mail-
ing list and you get
amazing catalogs of
flowers and bulbs.)

OCTOBER

To see the world in
a grain of sand,
And a Heaven in a
wild flower,
Hold Infinity in the
palm of your hand,
And eternity in an
hour.

—William Blake

OCTOBER

THE FIRST WEEK

GETTING READY

October is one of the greatest months of the year for gardeners. It is the month when all the green things are getting ready for cold weather. The leaves fall off the trees, weeds begin to turn yellow, and the earth is preparing to lie dormant for awhile.

This is the time when you can make money and help your garden at the same time. Ask your neighbors and your family if they will give you an allowance every week for raking their lawns. Ask if you can keep the leaves. Stuff as many leaves as you want into big plastic bags or make a pile of them where no one will mind.

Leaves are great for the soil. A big, fat layer of leaves on your garden will be rotted by springtime. Then you will be able to turn them under with a fork and plant new seeds. Leaves are one of Nature's best composts. Collect them now and you'll have better soil next summer.

LEAF MAGIC

Most parts of this country have a beautiful display of autumn color when the leaves get ready to fall off. Trees like the sumac and maple turn gold and then a fiery red before the leaves fall. Here is how it happens.

Abscission Layer

This is a maple leaf. In summer it is bright green. The sun is up and shining for long hours, and the plant uses its green chloroplasts to gather sunshine for energy to make food. Then as August begins, the sun shines for fewer and fewer hours. By October, the days are shorter. In November it is dark at dinner time and the sun comes up in the morning later than it does in July.

The tree doesn't get as much light in the autumn. This tells the plant that it is time to get ready for winter. With less light, the plant begins making certain substances, called hormones, which deliver messages to the leaves. The leaves grow special cells at the base of each stem. These cells are called the abscission layer, and they become weaker and weaker as the layer builds up. Finally this layer of cells is so weak that it falls apart, and the leaf drops off the tree.

As the abscission layer builds up, the green chlorophyll in the leaf gets old and breaks down. It gradually fades away. The red and yellow colors in a leaf increase and build up until the leaf is all yellow or red. The leaf turns brown when it isn't connected with the tree anymore. The leaf can't use the sun when the green chlorophyll is gone. It can't get water when the stem is broken. It dries up and becomes part of the soil. Now the tree is ready to rest until next Spring.

THE SECOND WEEK

HARVESTING

Many years ago, people waited with hope and fear for the end of the growing season. In September and October they would know whether they had enough food to last through the long, cold winter. It was hard to store food then. People couldn't just open a freezer or go to the grocery store when they needed food. If it wasn't growing in their fields, they would be hungry by springtime.

When fields of corn or wheat were being harvested, the whole village would pitch in so the crop wouldn't get rained on and spoil. Women, men, children, old, young, anyone who could walk helped in the harvest. The smallest children watched the babies. Older children ran behind the harvesters who were tying the grain into bundles, and picked up any grain that fell onto the

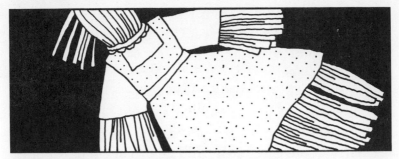

ground. When all worked, all would eat.

At last the fields would be cleared. The person who picked up the last bundle of wheat would cry out, "Here is the Harvest Child."

This was the signal for celebration. Everyone would gather around happily while someone tied the last bundle of wheat into a child-sized doll with arms, legs, body, and head made of bundles of grain. Sometimes this Harvest Child would be wrapped in cloth like a baby was or dressed in clothes.

The Harvest Child rode back to the village on the top of the last grain-loaded wagon. Then, when the grain had been put away for the winter, the Harvest Child was gently placed in the barn on top of the mounds of grain.

Cutting the wheat was taking the plant away from the earth. It was like when a baby is born out of its mother. The cord that connects the baby to the mother is cut when the baby is born. The baby doesn't mind. It is ready to begin its new life. The grain was cut away from its mother, the earth, so it was like a baby. The Harvest Child is the earth's baby. Having the Harvest Child was one of the ways that people celebrated the end of the gardening year.

How to Make a Harvest Child

You could make a Harvest Child. It would look great sitting on your porch, in a window, or in the middle of your garden space.

You can use cornstalks, dry weeds, and plants or a bundle of wheat if you can find some. Make legs and arms, a body. For a head you can use a pumpkin or a squash. Cut out eyes, nose, and mouth or cut paper ones out and glue them on. Cut a small hole in the bottom of the squash or pumpkin. Put one end of a dowel or stick in the hole. Put the long end of the stick down in the bundle of cornstalks that are the body and tie firmly.

You can dress your Harvest Child or leave it bare. Sometimes people made Harvest Mothers or Grandmothers. A cornstalk body, old dress, and pumpkin head with white cotton hair makes a great looking Harvest Grandmother.

Harvest figures are good to make for Halloween decorations.

THE THIRD WEEK

PUMPKIN PICKING

If you have pumpkins in your garden, you are about ready to pick them. Pumpkins last a long time in a cool place, so you can pick them now.

Pumpkins are very good to eat. Pumpkins can be stewed, dried, or fried, and they make a truly magnificent pie. Pumpkin seeds are delicious too. Here is a recipe for your seeds:

PUMPKIN SEED SNACK

Clean your pumpkin seeds in water. Get all the strings of pumpkin off. Then pat the seeds until they are nearly dry between two layers of towels.

Grease generously a big, flat pan with low sides. (Small pans like cake pans work fine, you just need more of them.) Pour the seeds into the pan to make a thin layer, not much more than one-seed deep.

Put the seeds in a 350° oven. Bake them about one half hour to one hour. Stir them occasionally. Take them out when they are golden brown. Sprinkle with salt. These are great alone or mixed with sunflower seeds and peanuts. Store them in cannisters or in tightly sealed plastic sacks.

CARVING A PUMPKIN

If you are making jack-o'-lanterns, be sure you have enough pumpkins. Everybody always likes to carve a jack-o'-lantern.

Put down a lot of newspapers. Scrape out the seeds with a spoon and save them to toast. It feels really nice to mush around with the pulp and seeds with your hands. Then wipe your hands and the pumpkin off.

You can draw a face on the pumpkin and then cut it or have someone cut it for you. I like to just dig in and begin. Cut whatever sort of face comes into your head. Let your hands design the face. Don't be discouraged if it doesn't look perfect. Some slips often make the best faces of all.

Remember, when you get a candle or small flashlight inside, all the faces look terrific.

THE FOURTH WEEK

THE END

Now it is the end. Your garden can be left alone until next Spring. It is your job to get the soil ready for winter and then leave the garden to rest while you go to school and do other things. It will be there again in the Spring. Next year it will be better than ever because now you know how to plant, to cultivate, to care for this piece of earth that is yours.

Begin by pulling up all the plants that are left in the garden. Chop or cut them up and scatter them over the dirt. They are full of minerals that will go back into the soil.

Did you collect leaves, hedge clippings, kitchen vegetable scraps? Pour them over the soil. Make a good thick layer. The winter rain and snow will pack it down quickly. You can add just about *anything* to this winter blanket. Hay, sand, manure, ashes from the fireplace or grill, seaweed, all these things make a good blanket for your garden. The more variety you add, the more minerals your garden will get. The leaves and old plants will decay and make a rich, crumbly soil for next year's garden.

On top of your mulch you can put your Harvest Child if you made one. It will sit there as the nights grow longer and colder until it also becomes part of the soil.

TOOLS

Your tools should be put away too. Wash and clean them well. Scrub off any rust with steel wool. Rub a light coating of mineral oil or linseed oil over the metal to protect it. Wrap the shovel, fork, and trowels in newspaper and put them where they will be dry during the winter.

Now your garden is at rest. It is always hard to believe, looking at the bare ground piled over with brown leaves and ashes, that beautiful, green plants can spring up from this place. Winter looks very final and cold as it begins, but you know that winter is just the first sign that Spring is coming.

MOMENTS

Looking back on it, I sometimes wonder why we garden. After all, there are plenty of farmers who will garden for us, and the groceries and florist shops are full of food and flowers to buy. It saves some money to grow our own vegetables and flowers, but it is often a lot of work and trouble too. I don't think that I garden just to save money or to use up my spare time.

Gardens are very special places, and that's probably why I like them. If you garden for years in one place, the garden will begin to look like you. It will be unlike any other person's garden. You can always tell the difference between a garden that has been loved and one where people gardened because they were paid a salary to do the work.

I think that the most beautiful gardens are always made from love. They aren't as neat and perfect sometimes as gardens in public parks where a crew of people work on the plants, but neatness isn't really that important in life. Most of the best things in life aren't very neat and perfect.

And there are moments, very strange and special moments when you are gardening. You work and work, spread manure and lay mulch, tie up tomatoes and water without seeing anything for days on end. Your garden seems a very ordinary place.

But then, suddenly, you bend over a squash plant, seeing deep into a yellow flower, and find yourself looking into the very eye of God.

INDEX

animals, 26-27
Aphrodite, 86
Arachne, 54-55
Athene, 54-55

beans, 60, 61, 83-84
  and Caddo legend, 82-83
  experiments with, 21-22, 41
  growing, 12, 94-95
bees, 21, 98-101
  pollination by, 98-99
birds, 28-30, 69, 86-87
Black Death, 18, 64
bulbs, onions, 43
  planting, 43-44

carrot(s), 60, 68-69, 109
  and zucchini dip, 133
catalogues, 144-46
catnip, 92-93
  tea, 93
celery, experiment with, 23
circle of life, 126, 141-43
clover, 20-21
Clytie, 85-86
compost, 50-51, 154-55
corn (maize), 17, 86-87
  Indians and, 24-26
Coyote Man, 48-50
cucumbers, 84
  experiment with, 84-85
  in gazpacho, 113

dandelions, 20
Demeter, 38-41
dirt (soil), 27-28
  preparation of, 62-63
dormancy, 15-16, 148

earthworms, 102-04
  experiments with, 104
  parts of, 102-03
evergreens, 15-16
experiments: with beans,
    21-22, 41
  with celery, 23
  with cucumbers, 84-85
  with light, 21-22

fertilizer, 125, 127
  compost as, 50-51, 154-55
flowers, 97-98, 101-02
foods, 26
foraging, 51-52

garden(s), 156-57
  in Autumn, 138-39, 154-55
  checklist for, 143-44
  choosing place of, 56-57
  club, 135-36
  digging the, 57-58
  history of, 10-11, 16-18
  journal, 12-13
  names for, 58
  plan, 60-62
  tools for, 155

garlic, 62, 63- 64
gastropod, 80
green, 135
    legend of Green Cup, 134-35

Hades, 39, 40
Hafiz, 101
harvest, 150-51
    Child and, 152, 155
heliotrope, 86
herbs, 90-93
Holy Grail, 134-35
hydrotropism, 23

Indians and legends, 23-26,
    48-50, 74-75, 82-83, 114-15,
    124-25
insects, helpful, 117-22
irrigation, 17

journal: of birds, 29
    of gardening, 12-13
    of trees, 52-53

kitchens, 32
    legend about, 32-33
    as seed store, 33

ladybugs, 117-20
leaf: in Autumn, 148-50
    collection, 52-53
    making food, 132
    parts of, 130-32
    and water, 133
legends, myths, and stories,
    23-24, 32-33, 34, 35, 38-41,
    48-50, 54-55, 65-66, 74-75,
    82-83, 85-86, 106, 109-10,
    114-15, 127-29, 134-35
lettuce, 79-80
light, 21-22

maize (*see* corn)
marigolds, 20
May Baskets, 70, 71
Mexico, 17
moon: phases of, 37
    planting by, 35-36
    stories about, 34-35
mulching, 95-97, 127

ocean, 18, 125-26
onions, 43, 60, 62, 63

pea(s): fairy tale of, 65-66
    growing, 60, 61, 67-68, 108-09
Persephone, 38-41
photosynthesis, 132
phototropism, 22
planting, 41-43, 56-57, 62-63
plant reproduction, 98
praying mantis, 120-22
Princess and the Pea, 65-66
pumpkins: carving, 153-54
    growing, 111-12, 152
    Jack-o'-lanterns, 110

radishes, 72
recipes: bean sprouts, 95
    catnip tea, 93
    gazpacho (drinking salad),
    113
    peppermint tea, 47

pumpkin seed snack, 153
sunflower seed snack, 88
zucchini and carrot dip, 133
rice, 17

seaweed, 126, 127
seeds, 12, 17, 33, 61, 97
snails, 80-82
Snake Woman, 82-83
snow, 13-14
spiders: myth about, 54-55
  helpfulness of, 55
  collecting webs, 56
Spring, 46-47, 69-70
Squanto, 124-25
squash: growing, 76-77
  legend of, 74-75
sunflowers, 87-88

thunder and lightning, 116
  legend of, 114-15
toads, 107-08

legend about, 106
tomatoes, 77-79
  in gazpacho, 113
turnips: growing, 130
  tale of, 127-29
trees, types of, 15-16

water, 22-23, 69, 116-17
  in leaf, 133
  table, 35-36
weather: experiment with
    beans, 41
  planting and, 41-43
weeds, 19-21, 95-96

Yellow Woman, 74-75
Yi, the archer, 106

Zeus, 40
zucchini, 77
  and carrot dip, 133